Presented To:

_____

From:

_____

Date:

_____

THE OVERCOMERS

BOOKS BY DR. RICHARD BOOKER

Discovering the Miracle of the Scarlet Thread in Every Book of the Bible

Celebrating Jesus in the Biblical Feasts

Radical Islam's War Against Christianity and the West

Living in His Presence

The Miracle of the Scarlet Thread Revised

Blow the Trumpet in Zion

AVAILABLE FROM DESTINY IMAGE PUBLISHERS

UNDERSTANDING THE BOOK OF REVELATION SERIES

THE OVERCOMERS

Dr. Richard Booker

DESTINY IMAGE® PUBLISHERS, INC.

P.O. Box 310, Shippensburg, PA 17257-0310

"Speaking to the Purposes of God for This Generation and for the Generations to Come."

This book and all other Destiny Image, Revival Press, MercyPlace, Fresh Bread, Destiny Image Fiction, and Treasure House books are available at Christian bookstores and distributors worldwide.

For a U.S. bookstore nearest you, call **1-800-722-6774.**

For more information on foreign distributors, call **717-532-3040.**

Reach us on the Internet: **www.destinyimage.com.**

ISBN 13 TP: 978-0-7684-3749-2

ISBN 13 Ebook: 978-0-7684-9006-0

For Worldwide Distribution, Printed in the U.S.A.

1 2 3 4 5 6 7 8 9 10 /15 14 13 12 11

Acknowledgments

TO Peggy, my wife and covenant partner of more than 45 years, who has faithfully served the Lord with me with unselfish love and support. Whatever I have been able to accomplish is because of her sacrifices and servant's heart. There are many great women in the world, but Peggy surpasses them all. She is the best Christian I know and a true overcomer.

I also want to thank my friends at Destiny Image, especially Don Nori, for being faithful to his vision of "speaking to the purposes of God for this generation and for the generations to come."

I want to acknowledge two of my students: Angela James, who gave so much of her time editing the manuscript, and Mark Sessions, who prepared the map and charts. Thank you both for your excellent work.

Contents

Preface

WHEN John was on the island of Patmos, the Lord gave him a revelation of Jesus, the exalted Son of Man, and of God's people overcoming satanic opposition and before the throne of God. In spite of tremendous persecution, John saw "in the Spirit" that the faithful followers of the Lord were victorious. They overcame satan by the blood of the Lamb and the word of their testimony. Furthermore, John was given revelation to see the spiritual warfare in Heaven that was being played out on the earth. He saw the outcome of this spiritual battle as well as prophetic events that would take place in the endtimes before the coming of the Lord.

John saw that God would totally and completely destroy His enemies and resurrect His own people to live with Him forever in a new Heaven, a new earth and a New Jerusalem. Regardless of the trials and tribulations God's people must endure, our destiny is certain and sure. Jesus is returning, and we will rule and reign with Him in a world free of satan, sin, and death. In the challenging days ahead, believers can joyfully commit their souls to God, who is faithful to keep His Word of promise.

As John wrote at the end of his vision:

And I heard a loud voice from heaven saying, "Behold, the tabernacle of God is with men, and He will dwell with them, and they shall be His people. God Himself will be with them and be their God. And God will wipe away every tear from their eyes; there shall be no more death, nor sorrow, nor crying. There shall be no more pain, for the former things have passed away" (Revelation 21:3-4).

So the Book of Revelation is not a book of doom and gloom, but of the victory of the Lamb and those who follow Him. The purpose of the Lord's revelation to John was to unveil or disclose to him what John could not know without divine assistance. The Lord gave John his vision to encourage and comfort his immediate readers as well as believers throughout the ages. What eventually became the Book of Revelation was clearly intended to be understood by John and his first-century readers.

However, with the passage of time, this book that God intended for us to understand became, without a doubt, the most mysterious book in the Bible. For almost 2,000 years, Christian scholars and everyday believers have tried to understand its message. Because the Book of Revelation is an apocalyptic vision filled with otherworldly symbols and descriptions of strange creatures, God's people have not always agreed on its meaning. This has led to a number of different interpretations of John's words.

Since there are so many books written on John's revelation, with so many different interpretations, why would I feel burdened to add to the confusion? It was certainly not my intention to write a book on the Book of Revelation. With more than 30 other books in print, I was ready to take a break from book writing. I wrote this book because there is an urgent need to explain John's revelation with the following four points of view that have not been adequately included in most commentaries on the Book of Revelation.

First, almost all books written to explain the Book of Revelation are written with a Western cultural worldview rather than a biblical worldview. There are some exceptions. What I mean by this is that the writer interprets the Book of Revelation through Western eyes rather than through the Hebraic eyes of a Middle Eastern person. John was not a Western theologian. He was a Jewish seer. This means that he understood and wrote his revelation in terms of his own history and culture. His history and culture is the Hebrew Bible—what Christians have always called the Old Testament. In this book, I prefer to use the phrase *Hebrew Bible.*

In order to understand the Book of Revelation, we must read it through the eyes of a Jewish man rather than through the eyes of a Western theologian. For example, when John sees Jesus in Heaven, he describes Him in Jewish terms, not Western Christian terms. To get the fullest meaning of John's vision of Jesus, we need to know Jesus, the Jewish "Son of Man." To John, Jesus is the "Cloud Man" of the Book of Daniel.

Second, since the Book of Revelation is the last book in the Bible, we must have a good understanding of all the other books in the Bible. We cannot understand the Book of Revelation if we do not have a good understanding of Genesis through Jude, as well as some basic knowledge of the literature written between the Testaments, and of Greek mythology. We must not read John's revelation as if it were written in modern times isolated from the rest of the Bible. The best way to understand the Book of Revelation is to begin with Genesis. For instance, when John explains the eternal home of believers in the last two chapters of the Book of Revelation, he assumes that the reader will be familiar with the first two chapters of the Book of Genesis.

Third, in order to understand the Book of Revelation, we must interpret it according to the type of literature John used in writing it.

John wrote the Revelation in an apocalyptic literary style. Apocalyptic literature flourished in the period of time in which John was writing. It has certain characteristics that John's readers readily understood. I explain these characteristics in Chapter 1. Because this is not a normal style of writing in our times, we have difficulty understanding and interpreting apocalyptic literature.

We have a tendency to interpret apocalyptic literature as if it were a literal story narrative, written chronologically like a Western textbook. Reading the Book of Revelation as a Western textbook can clearly lead us to wrong conclusions regarding John's statements. For example, when John says that he saw an open door into Heaven and heard a voice calling him to Heaven, he did not mean that he saw a literal door and was literally taken to Heaven. He meant that God opened his spiritual eyes so that he could see realities in Heaven that he would not know otherwise. Physically, John never left Patmos.

Fourth, to properly understand the Book of Revelation, we must know the historical context in which John wrote. Jesus gave John letters to write to seven literal congregations in the first century. Since the English word *church* means something different to modern readers than its biblical meaning, I use the word *congregation,* which is the more accurate meaning of the word. I could have used the words *assembly* or *community.* In a few instances, I use the word *Church* when referring to organized Christianity, such as the Roman Church or the Catholic Church. These congregations or communities were challenged every day to live out their new faith in a hostile environment in which their neighbors worshiped Greek gods and goddesses and Roman emperors, practiced gross immorality, and pressured them to compromise their faith and witness. They were faced with life-and-death decisions.

In addition, each of the cities where the seven congregations were located had their own unique physical circumstances that Jesus acknowledged in His letters. Without knowledge of their circumstances, spiritual and physical, it is impossible to understand why Jesus said what He said to the different congregations. For instance, if we do not know that Laodicea had a drinking water problem, we cannot understand why Jesus preferred the believers to be cold or hot rather than lukewarm.

I have the greatest appreciation for scholars and ministers who have spent years studying the Book of Revelation and have labored to help us understand its mysteries. While I present points of view in this book that most ministers and everyday believers might not be familiar with, I do not intend to be critical of what others have written or believe. We must all walk in love and humility and be gracious to one another, especially if we see things differently.

You may be challenged by some of my explanations that are contrary to your preconceived ideas and traditional teachings. You may not agree with everything I have written, and that is OK. What I desire to accomplish is to glorify our Lord, to encourage God's people to be steadfast and faithful as we face challenging days ahead, and to provide a fresh, exciting, and more balanced understanding of the Book of Revelation. If I accomplish these goals, I would be most grateful to our Lord. May God's people be blessed and His name praised forever.

For ease of reading and understanding, the publisher has wisely organized my writing on the Book of Revelation into a three-volume series entitled *Understanding the Book of Revelation*. Volume One is entitled *The Overcomers*. This volume begins with three chapters that are necessary for us to understand the historical events that prompted the Lord to send His letters to the seven congregations. In order to properly understand the Revelation, we must know the context in which it was written. I have also included a chapter on the literary style in which the book was written as well as a survey of the Book of Revelation. I then explain the letters to the seven congregations within their historical, geographical, archeological and Hebraic context and perspective along with my view of their prophetic and personal significance. This background information is often missing or not adequately explained in most books on the Revelation, but is critical to understanding the Revelation. Volume One covers Revelation 1-3.

Volume Two is entitled *The Lamb and the Seven-Sealed Scroll*. This volume opens up with John's vision of Heaven and the throne room of God. John sees the greatest drama in human history when the Lamb of God takes the seven-sealed scroll and opens the seals. I then explain the events that follow, including the opening of the first six seals, God's seal of protection, Israelites and Jews, the multitude of the redeemed, the opening of the seventh seal, the mighty angel and the little book, the two witnesses, the proclamation of the Kingdom of God, and the war in Heaven and on Earth. Volume Two covers Revelation 4-12. We will learn along the way that the Book of Revelation actually ends with the close of Revelation 11. The rest of the information is an "instant replay" giving more details and different looks at the same information.

Volume Three is entitled *The Victorious Kingdom*. This volume includes an explanation of the two false messiahs, a preview of the end, preparing to blow the seventh trumpet-shofar, the blowing of the seventh trumpet-shofar, the destruction of the one-world religious and political systems, the second coming of Messiah, the Battle of Armageddon, the Messianic Kingdom, the New Heaven and New Earth and Paradise Restored. Volume Three covers Revelation 13-22.

These volumes are designed to be read along with the Book of Revelation. Each discussion in the text is keyed to a specific chapter and verse in the Book of Revelation. To get the most from the text, first read the information in the Book of Revelation, and then read my explanations and comments in the books.

As I have already said, the Revelation is not a book about doom and gloom. While there are many hard things to read and much suffering in the book, Revelation is a book about God's faithfulness to Himself, His Word, and His people. It is about God defeating His enemies, and His people overcoming by the blood of the Lamb and the Word of their testimony. The outcome is certain and victory is sure. As you read the

Revelation and this three-volume series, may the Lord encourage your heart that our God is sovereign over world conditions and is using them to move forward His awesome plan of redemption for His people. Do not be fearful in the dark days ahead. We will live with our Lord forever in the full manifestation of His blazing glory and dazzling beauty. We will look upon Him as He is, for we shall be like Him.

Let us make the following prayer from Jude 24-25 our own personal praise and worship to our God:

> *Now to Him who is able to keep you from stumbling* [falling], *and to present you faultless before the presence of His glory with exceeding joy, to God our Savior, who alone is wise, be glory and majesty, dominion and power, both now and forever. Amen.*

Chapter 1

Understanding the Book of Revelation

OF all the books in the Bible, the Book of Revelation has been the most challenging to understand. In fact, it is the only book in the Bible about which the great reformer John Calvin refused to write a commentary. Throughout history, scholars have debated its meaning and how it should be interpreted. Some see it as having been written only for the believers who lived at the time John received his revelation. Others see it as a prophetic outline of Church history. Other scholars understand it only as a symbolic book explaining the spiritual battle of good against evil. More recently, scholars have interpreted Revelation as a book explaining only end-time events.

When discussing the Book of Revelation, Christians today argue about how to interpret the book, the meaning of its symbols, the identity of the anti-Messiah, the meaning of 666, the timing of the rapture, the nature of the millennial reign of Jesus, the timing of the Lord's return, and just about everything else in the book.

Million-seller books and movies are based on end-time prophecies from the Book of Revelation. While these books and movies are very popular with the Christian public, they often fail to present the Hebraic and cultural roots, historical background, and audience of the Book of Revelation. So it is vital that we do our best to understand John's words as his readers would have understood them. This may not be as exciting and sensational as the million-sellers, but this approach is more accurate.

The readers of John's message in the first century clearly understood what and who John was referring to in the symbols he used. But history and time and literary styles have obscured much of their meaning to us today. Christians need to realize that scholars who love the Lord and His Word have debated these subjects for centuries and come to different conclusions as to their meanings. This being the case, we should not think that we have all the answers and can explain ancient "otherworldly" visions and symbols with our fancy charts and diagrams.

We will continue to seek to understand the Book of Revelation and continue to disagree on much of what it means until Messiah comes. Because of this, we need to respect the views of others who have "seriously" studied the book and sought to understand it with sound scholarship and the help of the Holy Spirit.

We must not be arrogant and think we have all the answers, but rather present our views with a humble spirit and be open to considering the views of others. While it is good to share our insights, we certainly should not argue over our disagreements. Because that is all they are—disagreements. And we certainly should not make our views foundational doctrines that only divide us.

After all, the most important consideration in understanding the Book of Revelation is not that we all agree on the meaning of everything in the book. The most important consideration is that we understand that Jesus is Lord and King and Savior of all who put their trust in Him, and He is returning to establish His Kingdom on the earth. At that time, He will destroy evil, and His people will live with Him in a world of righteousness and peace.

Since this is the most important issue in the Book of Revelation, we should spend our time and energy learning how to prepare for His coming rather than arguing about things we don't clearly understand.

We should become great people of God and live as salt and light rather than great debaters who understand doctrine but don't love and serve people. With all this said, let's learn about the literary style of the Book of Revelation and see how scholars throughout history have sought to understand it. Let's do so with an open mind, a humble heart, and a teachable spirit. In other words, let's be willing to consider views that may be different from what we have always believed to be "the" one and only correct understanding of the Revelation.

APOCALYPTIC LITERATURE

In modern English, we have different types of literature such as technical documents, poems, fiction and nonfiction, etc. We realize that we don't interpret these different types of literature the same way. For example, we don't interpret a poem the same way we interpret a novel.

The Book of Revelation was written in a distinct literary style that is called "apocalyptic literature." Because this is not a normal literary style of writing in our modern era, we have difficulty understanding and correctly interpreting apocalyptic literature. However, it was a common style of writing in John's time, and people understood it and knew how to interpret it.

Apocalyptic literature as a writing style flourished in Jewish writings during times of great national distress. Its purpose was to encourage God's people that He had not forsaken them, and that in due time, He would judge their wicked oppressors and establish His Kingdom on the earth. In fact, in his book, *A Theology of the New Testament*, George Eldon Ladd calls apocalyptic literature "tracts for bad times."[1]

When the Jewish people were being persecuted and suffered at the hand of evil pagan rulers, they couldn't understand why God was allowing this to happen. Had He forsaken them? Was He really aware of their plight? Was He really the sovereign Lord over the evil rulers? Was He going to do something to help them? And if so, how and when? We have the same questions today.

One of the ways spiritual leaders sought to encourage the people was to give them an assurance of God's deliverance through apocalyptic writings. The central theme of these writings was that their God was indeed Lord of the world, that He did know of their sufferings, that He was allowing it for His own reasons that they did not understand, and that He would judge the evil rulers, deliver the people from their plight, and establish His Kingdom on the earth.

Apocalyptic literature had common characteristics. First, these books claimed to be a revelation from God. In fact, the Greek word for *apocalypse* means revelation, disclosure, or unveiling. The writer claimed to be revealing something he learned supernaturally from God that he was passing on to the people to encourage them in their time of despair. This is why the Book of Revelation is also referred to as the *Apocalypse*. So John begins his writing with the phrase, *"The Revelation of Jesus Christ"* [Yeshua the Messiah].

Second, apocalyptic literature is symbolic. The writer uses cosmic journeys, mysterious creatures, supernatural beings, strange, frightening beasts, numerology, etc., to explain invisible divine mysteries in the heavens in human terms for those living on the earth. The symbols were not intended to be understood literally, but represented real events and personalities that the readers would understand in their times.

For example, when John mentioned that Jesus has a sharp two-edged sword in His mouth (see Rev. 1:16), he didn't mean that literally. He meant that Jesus was speaking the creative *rhema* Word of God, as we learn from Hebrews 4:12-13.

Third, apocalyptic literature emphasizes the supernatural means of receiving the message and the supernatural intervention of God in human history. This literature commonly includes the writer in a spiritual state being transported to Heaven, or having visions on the earth where he sees the throne of God, and angelic beings that reveal to him the divine secrets and mysteries of the current political and religious situation on the earth. This includes God's future judgments and a new world order of God's Kingdom, with God's people being delivered from their suffering. All of these elements are in the Book of Revelation.

For example, in an apocalyptic book from the Apocrypha called First Enoch (1:9), we read that Enoch is taken by angels on a journey through the heavens and the realm of the dead. In the book, he relates what he saw and heard. In the Bible Book of Jude, the writer is actually referring to the book of Enoch and writes,

> *Now Enoch, the seventh from Adam, prophesied about these men also, saying, "Behold the Lord comes with ten thousands of His saints [angels], to execute judgment on all, to convict all who are ungodly among them of all their ungodly deeds which they have committed in an ungodly way, and of all the harsh things which ungodly sinners have spoken against Him"* (Jude 14-15). (See also Deuteronomy 33:2; Matthew 16:27; 25:31.)

In the Hebrew Bible, parts of the Books of Daniel, Ezekiel, and Zechariah are apocalyptic. These were difficult times when God's people were in exile in Babylon and struggling to reestablish themselves in Israel as well as looking into the future "last days."

Apocalyptic literature flourished in the period from Antiochus Epiphanes (164 B.C.) to the Bar Kochba revolt (A.D. 135) when Jews were suffering and fighting for their survival. Apocalyptic literature such as the Assumption of Moses, First Enoch, Fourth Ezra, the Apocalypse of Baruch and others, as well as Christian apocalyptic literature were plentiful and popular during the time that John wrote the Revelation. Believers were suffering at the hands of the Greeks and the Romans. They needed encouragement and assurance that God had not forsaken them and that righteousness would prevail. The point is that the people were familiar with the apocalyptic literary style and understood it.

While most of the Book of Revelation is apocalyptic, it also contains literal messages to seven literal congregations in Asia Minor (modern Western Turkey), and prophecy for our times. While it is a first-century book written to first-century believers, it is certainly appropriate for us today as believers face many of the same challenges. In fact, it seems like history is repeating itself. The central message is that God is in control of nations and world events, He will comfort His people in times of distress, and Jesus will return to Earth to judge the wicked and reward His own.

INTERPRETING REVELATION— HISTORICAL VIEWS

Throughout history, scholars have incorporated four different views in interpreting the Book of Revelation. Let's review each one.

The first of these views is called *preterism*. This is a strange word that comes from a Latin word that means before, previously or past tense. This method of interpreting Revelation is called by this name because scholars who embrace it believe that the events described in the Book of Revelation were fulfilled in the first century. To these scholars, the Book of Revelation is a history book only. Naturally, this view stresses the historical background of the Book of Revelation. It does not view the Revelation as prophetic.

This view was first taught in the 1600s by a Jesuit priest named Luis de Alcazar (1554-1613). In his time, the Protestant reformers claimed that Babylon and the political and religious messiahs in the Book of Revelation pointed to the Catholic Church and their persecution of the reformers. People, including ourselves, have a tendency to interpret the Book of Revelation based on their own time and circumstances. Because the Catholic Church was so powerful, yet so worldly and corrupt, and so evil in persecuting the reformers, it is easy to see how the reformers would identify the Beast of Revelation with the Catholic Church of their time. They were very successful in their presentation.

When Luis de Alcazar started teaching that the Book of Revelation was fulfilled in the first century and was not prophetic, he was countering the attack of the reformers against the Catholic Church. Since, in his view, the book was not prophetic, it couldn't be about the Catholic Church. In this way, he sought to nullify their attacks against the Catholic Church.

It is certainly true that John was writing to first-century believers to encourage them in their struggle against Rome. It was a time when worshiping the emperor was imposed on the people and believers who opposed it were martyred. We certainly must know this history in order to understand Revelation. But this view is self-serving and narrow with an agenda in that it only sees the Revelation as a history book with no prophetic significance throughout history or for the endtimes.

A second view of Revelation is called the *historical view.* This view interprets the Book of Revelation as a prophecy about the history of the organized Christian Church through time, from the first century to the return of Jesus.

In this approach, spiritual leaders of times past tried to identify specific nations, events, wars, and political and religious leaders in history with the Beast of Revelation, the symbols, the seals, the trumpets and the bowl judgments. The reformers clearly favored this view because they could identify the Beast with Rome and the political and religious system with the Catholic Church.

This is the view that has led to every generation claiming that the corrupt political leaders and religious leaders of their time were the ones John was writing about in the Revelation. Their conclusion was that they were the last generation and that the Lord would return in their lifetime.

While they were sincere in their attempts to understand the Revelation as it related to their time and circumstances, they always turned out wrong and could never rightly identify what person or events actually connected to those in the Revelation. Their conclusions always caused confusion because their speculations had to be far-fetched and constantly revised as they tried to identify events in history with the symbols in the Revelation. The anti-Messiah has been identified as everyone from Nero in the first century to Henry Kissinger in our times. This historical view might be more rightly called the *hysterical view* as it was constantly changing and causing confusion and turmoil.

Modern students of prophecy make the same error when they attempt to identify world leaders of our time with the Beast and False Prophet of Revelation. There are many in our day who have certain characteristics of those mentioned in the Revelation, and we should be alert to the signs of our times. But we must be cautious in saying, "This is that," or claiming that every corrupt politician and religious leader is the Beast and/or the False Prophet.

The third view of interpreting Revelation is called the *symbolic view* or *allegorical view.* Simply put, this view teaches that the Book of Revelation does not in any way refer to literal events in history, but is an allegory of the conflict between good and evil throughout history.

This view began at the first Christian Seminary in Alexandria, Egypt, with the teachings of Clement of Alexandria and his famous student, Origen. These were Greek scholars who embraced Jesus but wanted to disconnect Christianity from its Jewish roots. The way they did this was to interpret the Bible allegorically, which was the Greek way of interpreting text. In other words, they did not interpret the Bible literally. When we interpret the Bible allegorically, we lose the plain sense of the text and can make the Bible mean whatever we want it to mean.

The Alexandrian School of scholars was anti-Semitic and taught replacement theology. They could not accept a Jewish Jesus returning to Earth to rule as the Greater Son of David over a restored Israel. The allegorical view enabled them to "spiritualize" Revelation so that they would not have to accept a literal Messianic Kingdom of one thousand years.

Augustine (A.D. 354-430) proclaimed this view in his monumental work, *The City of God*. This was the view of the Christian Church world from the 5th century until the 16th century of the Puritans and Pilgrims who interpreted the Bible in its literal sense. While the Book of Revelation is filled with symbols which we are not to understand in their literal sense, they do represent literal events on the earth.

The fourth view of interpreting Revelation is called the *futurist view*. This is the view, and perhaps the only view, that most evangelical Christians today know about. In this view, Revelation is seen primarily as a book about the future. It is a book about Bible prophecy regarding the endtimes. Scholars who teach this view believe that everything after Revelation 4:1 to the end of the book is about end-time events just prior to and following the return of Jesus.

This is the view popularized by *The Late Great Planet Earth* and the *Left Behind* series. Since these books have been so influential, they have contributed to this view being held today by most evangelical Christians. This view understands that the first three chapters of Revelation were written to seven literal congregations in Asia Minor which also represent seven successive periods of Christian or "Church" history.

For example, Ephesus represents the apostolic Christian era that flourished from A.D. 33-100. Smyrna represents the persecuted Christian era from 100-312. Pergamos represents the compromising Christian era from 312-606. Thyatira represents the tolerant Christian era from 606-1517. Sardis represent the dead Christian era from 1517-1750. Philadelphia represents the faithful Christian era from 1750-1925. Finally, Laodicea represents the lukewarm Christian era from 1925 to the coming of the Messiah. However, there is really no solid reason for viewing the congregations of Revelation as representative of successive

Christian periods, because these types of congregations have existed in all periods of Christian history.

This view sees the believers as "caught up" or raptured and in Heaven in Revelation chapters four and five, with chapter six describing the beginning of end-time events on the earth. The futurist view is the most literal interpretation of the Revelation. It does try to make plain sense of the symbols, but runs the risk of understanding the symbols too literally. In other words, it does not adequately take into account the apocalyptic literary nature of the Revelation.

For example, there is no reason to believe that when John says that he was caught up into Heaven that this typifies the rapture of believers. John was not physically raptured to Heaven. John didn't go anywhere. He had a spiritual vision on the island of Patmos. It is simply an apocalyptic way of expressing the divine origin of the Revelation. To say that he represents the Church is a fanciful imagination.

Which of these views is correct? They all have some element of truth. The challenge in embracing any one of the views is to think that it is the *only* view and that the others are to be criticized and ignored. We can learn from all of these views while not taking any of them to the extreme.

For example, it is important to learn as much as we can about the historical situation when John wrote the Revelation. But if we only view the Revelation as a history book, it has little or no relevance for us today. It is also helpful to understand how world history and Christian history have clashed through the ages. But this leads to prophetic speculation and confusion where we try to identify any and every world and religious leader with the frightening figures and symbols in the Revelation.

It is good to understand that the Revelation tells us about the war in Heaven between good and evil, the allegorical view. But the symbols were more than just an allegory. They represent real places, people, and events on the earth. The futurist view certainly helps us understand the plain sense of the Revelation but, taken to an extreme, can read into the text too literal of an interpretation.

The best approach is to understand the Revelation as apocalyptic literature written to seven literal congregations at the close of the first century. The readers would have understood the meaning of the symbols for their time. While the events that John described were about a real historical conflict between Roman imperial cult worship and the believers in Western Asia, they also foreshadow the spiritual war between good and evil down through the ages that will culminate in the endtimes with the coming of the Lord, who will destroy evil and establish a literal Kingdom on the earth.

INTERPRETING REVELATION— END-TIME VIEWS

In addition to these four historical views of understanding the Revelation, there have been three different views of the endtimes all based on a different interpretation of one passage of Scripture in Revelation. These three views are: 1) postmillennialism, 2) amillennialism, and 3) premillennialism. Don't let these big words confuse you, because I am now going to explain what they mean.

The passage of Scripture that theologians debate is Revelation 20:1-6, which reads:

> *Then I saw an angel coming down from heaven, having the key to the bottomless pit and a great chain in his hand. He laid hold of the dragon, that serpent of old, who is the devil and satan, and bound him for a thousand years; and he cast him into the bottomless pit, and shut him up, and set a seal on him, so that he should deceive the nations no more till the thousand years were finished. But after these things he must be released for a little while.*

And I saw thrones, and they sat on them, and judgment was committed to them. Then I saw the souls of those who had been beheaded for their witness to Jesus and for the word of God, who had not worshiped the beast or his image, and had not received his mark on their foreheads or on their hands. And they lived and reigned with Christ [Messiah] *for a thousand years.*

But the rest of the dead did not live again until the thousand years were finished. This is the first resurrection. Blessed and holy is he who has part in the first resurrection. Over such the second death has no power, but they shall be priest of God and of Christ [Messiah], *and shall reign with Him a thousand years.*

The postmillennial view is that Christianity will establish the Kingdom of God on the earth, at which time the Lord will return. This view does not interpret the thousand years as literal, but spiritualizes it to mean an indefinite period of time in history when God's people will fully establish the Kingdom of God on the earth. When Christianity has completed this mission, it will invite Jesus to return to a world that is sanctified and eagerly awaiting His return.

Augustine developed this view in his famous work, *The City of God*, and established it as the end-time theology from the 5th century to the 15th century. As the Roman Empire was crumbling and as barbarians were destroying the existing order, Augustine taught that the Roman Church, meaning organized Christianity, was the "City of God" that would take the empire's place and grow in power to the point that it would rule the world. Augustine also taught that the Roman Church, as the "City of God," was the same as the Kingdom of God.

This view of the millennium gave a theological justification for the Roman Church to forcefully extend its political and religious rule and authority by political alliances and conquests. The fact that Christianity became the official religion of the empire and survived and flourished when the empire crumbled gave credibility to Augustine's teachings. They believed Roman Christianity would convert the world.

During the 1800s, Christian nations colonized much of non-Christian Africa and Asia. This opened the door for missionaries to take the Gospel to these countries. To the Christians of that era, it seemed like they would soon establish Christian rule over the nations, which would usher in the coming of the Lord. It was an exciting time for missionary work, and there was great optimism.

But aside from this view not being scriptural, the Bible says that the world will get *more* evil, not less (see 2 Tim. 3:1-5). World War I put an end to the belief that the world was getting better. The modern terms for postmillennialism are "Kingdom Now" and "Dominion Theology." While this is still the official doctrine of many of the historic denominations, it should be clear to anyone that Christianity is not going to convert the world.

Augustine was also a proponent of amillennialism. As mentioned earlier, his method of interpreting the Bible was allegorical. This means he spiritualized the prophecies about the Kingdom of God, the millennium, the tribulation, Christianity and the Jews, and end-time events in general. According to his view, the end-time prophecies are not to be taken literally.

If you accept Augustine's writings, you believe that you are now living in the millennial Kingdom of God on the earth, which is Christendom, as a citizen of the New Jerusalem, which is spiritual. The devil is effectively bound, and you are establishing God's rule over the earth. Wow, that is too much for even the most optimistic, positive-thinking believer.

This spiritualized view of Christianity was manifested by Christian dominance of the Jews who were to be forever humiliated and disgraced. Augustine wrote that the Jews deserved death, but instead they were to wander the earth as a witness to their punishment and the victory of

Christianity over the synagogue. Augustine's writings became the theological textbook for Christianity for 1,000 years, and his views are still taught by much of the Christian world. No wonder anti-Semitism is still rampant in Christianity.

Premillennialism takes a literal view of the end-time prophecies. This view is that Jesus will return before the millennium, at which time the Lord will bind satan and set up His Messianic Kingdom on the earth, with His saints ruling and reigning with Him for a literal thousand years.

While we can understand how theologians of the past arrived at their views, in the light of history and our modern world, the view of prophecy in the Hebrew Bible, and the restoration of Israel and prophetic signs of the times, the premillennial view is the only view that is consistent with the plain sense of Scripture and redemptive history.

REVIEW QUESTIONS

1. Write a summary of what you have learned in this lesson. Write the summary in clear, concise words as if you are going to present it to another person.

2. Write an explanation of how you can apply what you have learned in this lesson to your life.

3. Share what you have learned with your family, friends, and members of your study group.

ENDNOTE

1. George Eldon Ladd, *A Theology of the New Testament* (Grand Rapids, MI: Eerdmans, 1993), 671.

Chapter 2

Background to the Book of Revelation

REVELATION REVIEW

IN the first chapter, we noted the many different views that scholars have of the Book of Revelation. While the first-century believers to whom John wrote clearly understood his message, the apocalyptic style of writing, time, and history have obscured much of its meaning to us today.

Because the Western Christian mind seeks knowledge rather than holy living, we spend more time debating the meaning of the Revelation of Jesus than we do preparing for His coming. We should want to understand the Revelation, not so we can have pride of learning and argue over the meaning of the symbols and details, but to know how to prepare ourselves for godly living. This is particularly critical in light of the message the book has for our times and personal life.

As I explained, the Book of Revelation was written in a style of writing which is unfamiliar to us today. However, it was a writing style that flourished in Jewish and early Christian writings from about 200 B.C. to A.D. 150. This was during times when God's people were suffering persecution at the hand of evil pagan rulers. The believers needed assurance that God had not forsaken them, that He would judge the ungodly, establish His righteous Kingdom on the earth, and that His people would overcome in the end.

The purpose of apocalyptic literature was to give them this assurance. The writer claims to have been in a spiritual state, at which time he received a supernatural revelation from God. He used symbols and "otherworldly" language to explain heavenly activities that were manifested on the earth through real events and personalities that the readers would understand.

In his monumental work, *The City of God*, Augustine established the allegorical interpretation of Scripture and end-time prophecies. His views would prevail from the 5th to the 15th centuries until the time of the Pilgrims and the Protestant Reformation.

As the Roman Empire was crumbling, and as barbarians were destroying the existing order, Augustine taught that the organized Roman Church was the "City of God" that would take its place and grow in power to the point that it would rule the world. Augustine also taught that the organized Roman Church was the same as the Kingdom of God.

This view of the endtimes gave a theological justification for the organized Roman Church to forcefully extend its political and rule and authority through political alliances and conquests. The result was a spiritual catastrophe as Rome replaced Jerusalem, the Pope replaced Jesus, and the organized Roman Church replaced Israel. This form of replacement theology and interpretation of the Book of Revelation was directly responsible for promoting ant-Semitism as official Roman Church and Christian doctrine.

Today, we have the benefit of hindsight to see the error of Augustine and others who completely spiritualized the Book of Revelation. The Book of Revelation can best be understood as a unique book that mixes literal messages to real congregations with apocalyptic symbols not to be understood in the literal sense.

The end-time message is that God is in control of world events and that He has not forgotten nor forsaken His people. In His appointed time, a real Jesus will return to a real Earth and defeat a real devil and his world system. Jesus will reign over a real world as King of kings and Lord of lords.

While trials of our faith, suffering, and tribulation are inevitable when God's Kingdom clashes with the kingdoms of the world, we have the assurance of God's faithfulness to His Word. His people will overcome and reign with Him forever. Hallelujah!

With this brief review, let's now discover the situation in the Roman world of the first century to learn the background and purpose for John receiving and writing the Revelation.

ROMAN EMPEROR WORSHIP

In the ancient pagan world of the Romans, people worshiped many gods. They believed particular deities ruled over and controlled different aspects of nature and their individual lives. Not only did each nation have many gods, villages had their own local deities, as did individual households. The people looked to these gods for protection and provision. They feared their wrath and sought to appease them by making sacrifices.

As Rome came to power and extended its empire, it came into contact with the gods of other cultures and religious beliefs. The Romans were happy to embrace new foreign gods and customs as long as this contributed to their ever-widening influence, power, and control of the people.

Rome went so far as to build temples and establish priesthoods to these foreign gods in Rome itself. To Rome, the more gods the better. Sometimes they kept the foreign names of the adopted deities, such as the Persian god Mithra, and other times they changed their names to Latin. For example, Zeus (Greek) became Jupiter (Latin).

Much like in America where the Senate and the President fight each other for control, the Roman senate and the emperor did the same. Eventually, under Julius Caesar (49-44 B.C.), the emperor got the upper hand.

With the establishment of an imperial system ruled by the emperor, Roman religion added another deity, the emperor himself. This not only contributed to the ego of the emperor, but it was a major factor in unifying the empire.

Imperial cult emperor worship with its accompanying sacrifice to the emperor was the required test of loyalty to the empire. Generally, the emperor was only declared a god at his death. But others, such as Domitian, demanded worship while they were still alive. This system of emperor worship would continue throughout the empire until Constantine stopped it.

Rome did not care how many gods the people worshiped as long as the emperor was on the list. This requirement of emperor worship became the main source of conflict between the first-century believers and Rome.

Because the believers would not worship the emperor, the Roman government considered them to be atheists. They didn't ask the believers to deny their faith, but simply to add the emperor to their devotion. It was not a problem for non-believers to add the emperor to their list of gods. But for those who worshiped the One True God and Him alone, emperor worship was not possible.

As believers refused to worship the emperor as a god, they would be persecuted. This is the background to the reason why John received the Revelation, wrote it, and distributed it to the Christian believers.

The Romans had a great ceremony marking the transition of the emperor to divine status. Each year, this glorious occasion would be remembered by making sacrifices to the emperor. Whenever called upon to do so, loyal subjects made sacrifices to the emperor at his temple and statue. They received a certificate that was their proof of loyalty.

As the first absolute ruler of the empire, Julius Caesar was the first to claim himself a descendant of the gods. Even before his death, a temple was dedicated to him with the name, "Jupiter Julies." His statue, erected a year before he died, was inscribed with the words, "To the invincible god." This was all just too much for some in the senate. So on March 15, 44 B.C., two leading members of the senate, Cassius and Brutus, assassinated Julius Caesar. "Beware the ides of March" became a famous saying relating to this event.

Octavian, Julius Caesar's nephew and adopted son, was appointed as the new Caesar (27 B.C.–A.D. 14). Octavian was given the title of "Augustus" by the senate. He gradually got all the power into his own hands. As the son of "the invincible god," Augustus not only accepted but actively promoted the cult of emperor worship. But he didn't wait until he died to accept the adoration of the people. He built temples, statues, and celebration events in his honor throughout the empire. This included Asia Minor where he built a temple to himself in Pergamos. When he died, the senate conducted the official ceremony proclaiming Augustus as one of the Roman gods.

Later emperors such as Tiberias (A.D. 14-37), Claudius (A.D. 41-54), Vespasian (A.D. 69-79), and Titus (A.D. 79-81) maintained the imperial cult of emperor worship but did not actively promote it. But three emperors believed their own "press releases" and actively promoted it with a fanatical zeal.

Caligula (A.D. 37-41) declared himself to be a god. In A.D. 40, he ordered his statue to be placed in the Temple in Jerusalem. This would be the worst imaginable *"abomination of desolation"* to the Jewish people.

The Roman governor overseeing Judea at that time realized that if he carried out this order, all of Judea would riot. He begged Caligula to rescind his order. At the request of his childhood friend, Herod Agrippa I, Caligula agreed to delay the order, but demanded that the governor of Judea kill himself. Fortunately for the governor and the Jews, the Praetorian Guard assassinated Caligula before the order could be carried out.

Nero (A.D. 54-68) was an insecure egomaniac who needed to be worshiped. He claimed a miraculous and divine birth. The Roman high god was the sun god. When Nero built a temple for sun worship, he put his own face on the statue representing the sun god.

Nero desired to build a great palace to his own honor. However, Rome was overbuilt. In A.D. 64, a fire of curious origin burned a major part of Rome, specifically in the area where Nero wanted to build his palace. The people blamed Nero for the fire. Nero shifted the blame by accusing the Christians of starting the fire. Nero was forced to commit suicide in A.D. 68.

Since his suicide was in private, many of the general public did not believe he was really dead. Some thought he would reappear or be resurrected. Since some believe his name equals the numeric value of 666, Nero was considered by certain groups to be the first anti-Messiah.

Nero inflicted horrible sufferings on the believers. He covered them with skins of wild beasts so dogs would tear them to pieces. He used them as human torches in his garden at night by fastening them to crosses and setting them on fire. He sent them to die in the Coliseum and subjected them to many other cruel and inhumane deaths.

Most scholars believe that Paul was martyred in Rome by Nero between A.D. 62 and 64. The organized Catholic Church teaches that Peter was also martyred in Rome at this time.

Some believe that Hebrews 11:35-40 may be referring to this terrible time of persecution. It reads:

> *Women received their dead raised to life again. Others were tortured, not accepting deliverance, that they might obtain a better resurrection. Still others had trials of mockings and scourgings, yes, and of chains and imprisonment.*

They were stoned, they were sawn in two, were tempted, were slain with the sword. They wandered about in sheepskins and goatskins, being destitute, afflicted, and tormented—of whom the world was not worthy.

They wandered in deserts and mountains, in dens and caves of the earth. And all these, having obtained a good testimony through faith, did not receive the promise, God having provided something better for us, that they should not be made perfect apart from us.

So much was happening during this time that greatly impacted the world of Rome, the Jews, and the Christians. For example, when Nero burned Rome in A.D. 64, he blamed the Christians and persecuted them unmercifully. The first Jewish revolt against the Romans was in A.D. 66 and lasted until A.D. 73. Nero died in A.D. 68. Titus destroyed Jerusalem and burned down the Temple in A.D. 70. If this was not enough, something just as frightening was about to take place that would influence the Christian world forever.

DOMITIAN

This brings us to the Emperor Domitian, whose actions to force those in the empire to worship him provide the setting for the Book of Revelation. Who was Domitian and why did he promote emperor worship? To understand his motives and actions requires some knowledge of his family.

In A.D. 66, the Jews revolted against Roman rule in what became known as the First Jewish War. At that time, General Vespasian was sent to Judea to put down the revolt. His son, Titus, accompanied him and was in charge of the famed Tenth Legion. They had almost ended the revolt when they heard that Nero died. Nero died without a clear successor. This led to a civil war, with four different generals declaring themselves emperor in A.D. 69.

Vespasian and Titus stopped fighting against the Jews and waited for further orders. Finally, Vespasian was recalled to Rome where he became emperor from A.D. 69-79. Titus stayed in Judea and finally ended the Jewish revolt by burning Jerusalem and the Temple in A.D. 70. The famous "Arch of Titus" still stands today in Rome as a monument to his triumph.

For the next ten years, Vespasian ruled the world and continued the imperial cult of emperor worship. He shared much of his glory with his son, Titus.

Both Vespasian and Titus practically ruled the empire together. Titus was like the co-emperor with his father. They received all the glory and adoration of the empire. So when Vespasian died in A.D. 79, Titus succeeded him as emperor from A.D. 79-81.

Meanwhile, Vespasian's younger son, and brother to Titus, Domitian, was overlooked and ignored. He spent his early years living in the shadow of his famous brother. Later, he was given ceremonial titles but no real responsibilities befitting the son and brother of the emperor. But this was about the change. When Titus died of a mysterious illness, Domitian was declared emperor. He ruled for 15 years (A.D. 81-96).

Domitian devoted the early part of his reign to consolidating his power, establishing himself as emperor, and administering the empire. But in the last half of his reign (A.D. 90-96), his emphasis changed to promoting the imperial cult of emperor worship.

Domitian insisted on being called "the lord god" and even issued coins bearing this phrase. In addition, he decided to build a statute and altar to himself in Ephesus, in the Roman province of Asia Minor. The seven congregations in Revelation were located in Asia Minor.

The Romans built a temple or statue and altar to the emperor in every province as a way of unifying the empire and testing the loyalty of the citizens. As we just learned, Asia Minor already had a temple to the emperor in Pergamos. Now, Domitian was going to build a second image and altar in Asia Minor at Ephesus. Asia Minor would now have two locations dedicated to emperor worship.

The place of imperial worship had a statue of Domitian and an altar where citizens of Ephesus were required to bow in worship to the image of Domitian as lord god. Those who refused were either exiled or put to death. Some believers hoped to pretend to bow to the emperor by bending over to fix their sandals when they got to the front of the statute. In other words, they didn't want to bow to the image but did not have the courage not to.

The Jews asked their rabbis if this was an acceptable thing for them to do. After all, they didn't really mean to bow down to the emperor, but they didn't want to die or be exiled. The question was, "Can a Jew fix his sandals in front of a pagan altar?" The rabbis ruled that a Jew could not fix his sandals (pretend to bow down) in front of a pagan statue, even if they said the *Shema* while doing so. Christian believers came to the same conclusion. Many scholars believe it was this decision by Domitian that caused John to be exiled to Patmos and his receiving the Revelation.

Why was it so important to the Romans that the Jews and followers of Jesus bow down to the emperor? Why did they exile or kill those who refused?

As previously noted, the imperial cult of emperor worship was a way of uniting the empire and proving the loyalty of the people. The Romans didn't care how many gods the people had, as long as they included the emperor. Bowing down to the emperor was more of a political statement than a religious one. It was showing allegiance to Rome and the Roman system as your lord and god.

The emperor represented the empire. Even though the senate still operated in Rome, the emperor ruled the empire. Rome was a dictatorship and the emperor was the dictator.

Bowing down to the statue of the emperor showed allegiance to Rome. This meant the whole Roman way of life, including its government, its policies, decrees and rulings, its institutions, its culture and values. If you wanted to live, you did not have a choice. You did not have freedom of worship and conscience.

Rome began as a republic, a government of leaders representing the people. But it became a totalitarian regime, a political system that was intolerant of dissent. If you refused to bow down to the emperor, you were considered anti-Roman, a disloyal citizen. You were either exiled or killed.

Early on, Jews and the followers of Jesus believed and accepted the idea that they would rather die for their faith than compromise. This is the background to the Book of Revelation.

ROME AND AMERICA

Like Rome, America also began as a republic, but with a difference. The American republic was established based on the laws of God in the Bible. America is the only nation in the history of nations that was birthed out of religious persecution and with a Judeo-Christian worldview and vision.

It is this Judeo-Christian heritage that has made America great. The Pilgrims and Puritans came to America because of religious persecution by the State Church of England. They were godly people who saw themselves establishing a colony in the new world that would be a shining light of God's redemption to the nations.

Before they landed, the Pilgrims wrote the Mayflower Compact which was their covenant they would live by as a colony. It was modeled on the covenant of their separatist congregation in England. They clearly stated that they came to the new world for the glory of God and the advancement of the Christian faith. Whether one likes it or not, the record is clear that the Pilgrims intended to establish America as a Judeo-Christian republic based on the Bible. When our founding fathers gathered to write and publish the Declaration of Independence, they couldn't agree among themselves. Finally, Benjamin Franklin stood and addressed the assembly with these words:

> I have lived, sir, a long time, and the longer I live, the more convincing proofs I see of this truth: that God governs in the affairs of men. If a sparrow cannot fall to the ground without His notice, is it probable that an empire can rise without His aid? We have been assured in the sacred writings that unless the Lord builds the house, they labor in vain who build it. I firmly believe this, and I also believe that without His concurring aid, we shall succeed in this political building no better than the builders of Babel.[1]

The founding fathers concluded the Declaration of Independence with these words:

> And for the support of this declaration, with a firm reliance on the protection of the Divine Providence we mutually pledge to each other, our lives, our fortunes and our sacred honor.

John Adams, second President of the United States said:

> We have no government armed with power capable of contending with human passions unbridled by morality and religion. Our Constitution was made only for a moral and religious people. It is wholly inadequate to the government of any other.[2]

Most of the founders of America made similar statements acknowledging the sovereignty of God, their Judeo-Christian worldview and values, and the Bible as the basis for our laws. Our Ivy League colleges and universities were established for the primary purpose of educating Christian ministers, and many of its earliest graduates were ministers.

The founding fathers stated that the American republic was designed for a moral people and would not survive unless there was a moral consensus of the citizens. While America has been a great light to the nations, our light has grown dim because we have abandoned our Judeo-Christian heritage. Born as a self-governing people under the moral laws of God, America now despises the laws of God and flaunts its immorality in the face of God, as if we dared Him to judge us.

The consequence of such actions is clear to anyone who has eyes to see. After hurricane Katrina devastated New Orleans, someone from New Orleans asked a well-known Christian leader the question, "Where was God? Why did He allow this to happen?" The person gave a very wise answer and said, "We expelled God from school. We voted Him out of our political system. We dismissed Him from our judicial system. We told Him we didn't want Him involved in our lives. And we wonder why He allowed this? God doesn't go where He is not wanted."

I think we can all agree that, in spite of the fact that the great majority of Americans profess faith in God and Christianity, our leaders in government, business, education, the press, and other critical structures of our society do not want the rule of God. As a result, they are building a tower of Babel that Benjamin Franklin warned against.

As America abandons its Judeo-Christian heritage, the nation becomes more lawless because the people are not able to govern themselves. As the nation becomes more lawless, the federal and state governments pass more laws to control the behavior of the citizens. Government intrudes into every area of our lives. Instead of relying on Divine Providence, people start relying on the government. It is not long before the republic becomes a dictatorship based on a personality cult.

Unless there is some late great spiritual awakening, America will soon become a totalitarian regime; that is, a political system that is intolerant of dissent. It will take away the basic rights guaranteed by the Constitution. There will be no free speech, no freedom of worship, and no right to bear arms. The government will dictate every area of our lives. The local "community organizers" will become the local government spies reporting those who do not bow down to the government. We will be required to have a "Certificate" (Mark of the Beast?) to verify our loyalty to the state.

As nations merge their national identities into the new world order, history will repeat itself. Once again, believers are facing a one-world totalitarian political-religious-economic system that will force people to accept its policies or be persecuted.

In America, it is the people of God who believe in the Bible who will be the dissenters. Our traditional moral values based on the Bible that made this nation great are being slandered and ridiculed. If you refuse to bow down to the anti-Judeo-Christian policies of the government, you will be considered anti-American, a disloyal citizen, an enemy of the state. *"He who has an ear, let him hear..."* (Rev. 2:7).

JESUS OR CAESAR

What does God say to His people in such difficult times? I want to conclude this chapter by giving four things I believe God would say to us when faced with the choice of bowing down to a modern day Domitian.

1. Do not love the world.

First, do not love the world. First John 2:15-17 reads:

> *Do not love the world or the things in the world. If anyone loves the world, the love of the Father is not in him. For all that is in the world—the lust of the flesh, the lust of the eyes, and the pride of life—is not of the Father but is of the*

*world. And the world is passing away, and the lust of it;
but he who does the will of God abides forever.*

When John says "love not the world," he doesn't mean God's created universe, but the world system that is anti-God. The Bible says in
numerous places that satan is the god of this world system in which we
live (see 2 Cor. 4:4; Eph. 2:2; John 12:31; 14:30). First John 5:19 says that
"...the whole world lies in the sway of the wicked one."

Through his powerful lies and deception, satan has established a
world system that expresses his own philosophies, attitudes, attractions,
ways, and means to draw people away from the One True God. Satan
seeks to be worshiped as god through his world system.

The Roman Empire was certainly an anti-God system. Bowing
down to the emperor was acknowledging your devotion and loyalty
to the Roman world system. Not only could you not advance in the
empire, you couldn't live unless you bowed to the emperor.

Our world system today is still ruled over by the evil one. It is the
same spirit that demanded emperor worship. If our desires and priorities, reflected by the way we spend our time and money, are for the
things of the world, we will not be able to stand against the Domitians
of our day. Just like believers in the first century, we are now being faced
with this choice.

2. Do not imitate the world.

The second thing I believe the Lord would say to us today is "Do not
imitate the world." Paul was a Roman citizen who could have made it
big in the Roman world. Instead he wrote:

*I beseech you therefore, brethren, by the mercies of God,
that you present your bodies a living sacrifice, holy, and
acceptable to God, which is your reasonable service. And
be not conformed to this world, but be transformed by the*

renewing of your mind, that you may prove what is that good and acceptable and perfect will of God (Romans 12:1-2).

The world of Paul's day was a Roman world. Like our world today, it was anti-God. There is a famous phrase that says, "When in Rome, be like the Romans." Paul is saying, "No—don't be like the Romans." Don't conform to this world. Don't imitate it. Don't copy it. Don't take on its values, its priorities, its entertainment, its way of speaking, its way of dress, etc. We are to be in the world but not of the world. We are to imitate the Lord, not the world. We are to live as the moral and spiritual salt and light of the world (see Matt. 5:13-16).

3. Dedicate yourself totally to God.

The third thing I believe the Lord would say to us today is to dedicate ourselves totally to Him. As we have learned, in the first century, people had to acknowledge Caesar as lord. This was a life or death decision on their part. To nonbelievers, it meant nothing to add Caesar to their existing gods. But for the believer, only Jesus is Lord.

Our faith is now being put to the test. We are all being challenged with the question, "Who is our Lord? Caesar or Jesus?" If we have settled that beforehand, we will be able to stand firm no matter the consequences. God will give us the grace to acknowledge Him as Lord. But if we haven't totally made that commitment to Him now, when the time comes, we may be tempted to "fix our sandals" when bowing before the modern Caesars of our world.

4. Commit your soul to God.

Finally, I believe the Lord would say to us today to commit our souls to Him. In John 15:18-20, Jesus said:

> *If the world hates you, you know that it hated Me before it hated you. If you were of the world, the world would love its own. Yet because you are not of the world, but I chose you out of the world, therefore the world hates you. Remember the word that I said to you, "A servant is not greater than his master." If they persecuted Me, they will also persecute you.* (John 15:18-20)

The Roman world of the first century hated Jesus. The new world order of our times still hates Jesus. Since He is not here in person to persecute, the empires of our world today show their hatred of God by persecuting His people.

Be that as it may, Jesus said, *"Let not your heart be troubled; you believe in God, believe also in Me"* (John 14:1). He further added in John 16:33, *"These things I have spoken to you, that in Me you may have peace. In the world you will have tribulation; but be of good cheer, I have overcome the world."*

Peter wrote, *"Therefore let those who suffer according to the will of God* [for righteousness sake] *commit their souls to Him in doing good, as a faithful Creator"* (1 Pet. 4:19).

God is a faithful Creator. He has promised us that His grace for our lives will always be with us in greater measure than any demand the world system may make on us. If we endure, we will overcome by the blood of the Lamb and the word of our testimony.

Paul suffered and died at the hands of the Roman Empire. While the beast of Rome murdered Paul, all the Roman emperors are dead; yet, 2,000 years later we are still reading Paul's letters. He wrote from firsthand experience for our encouragement:

> *Yet in all these things we are more than conquerors through Him who loved us. For I am persuaded that neither death nor life, nor angels nor principalities nor powers, nor*

things present nor things to come, nor height nor depth, nor any other created thing, shall be able to separate us from the love of God which is in Christ [Messiah] *Jesus our Lord* (Romans 8:37-39).

As we face challenging days ahead, let us examine ourselves. Do we love the Lord more than the things of the world? Are we imitating the Lord or the world? Have we fully dedicated ourselves to God and Jesus as King and Lord of our lives, or do we just know Him as Savior? Have we resolved to faithfully commit our souls to the Lord regardless of the consequences? We must settle these issues in our lives now. Let us be firm in our faith. Let us not compromise and seek to "fix our sandals" before the anti-God world.

REVIEW QUESTIONS

1. Write a summary of what you have learned in this lesson. Write the summary in clear concise words as if you are going to present it to another person.

2. Write an explanation of how you can apply what you have learned in this lesson to your life.

3. Share what you have learned with your family, friends, and members of your study group.

ENDNOTES

1. Nancy Leigh DeMoss, editor, *The Rebirth of America*, (Philadelphia: Author S. DeMoss Foundation, 1986), 31.2. Letter to the Officers of the First Brigade of the Third Division of the Militia of Massachusetts (11 October 1798).

2. The Works of John Adams (U.S. diplomat and politician 1735-1826), Charles Francis Adams, ed., *The Works of John Adams, Second President of the United States, 1854*, 9:229. (October 11, 1798).

Chapter 3

Survey of the Book of Revelation

REVELATION REVIEW

WE have learned that John wrote the Revelation as apocalyptic literature. This type of literature uses symbols and "otherworldly" visions and language to communicate heavenly realities to people living on the earth. This is not a common form of literature to modern readers.

While most of the Book of Revelation is symbolic, it also contains literal messages to seven literal congregations in Asia Minor (modern Turkey), plus prophecy for our times. While first-century believers would have clearly understood John's message, it is not as clear to us today. This has led to many interpretations of the Revelation.

The event that seems to have prompted John to write his revelation was associated with emperor worship. Rome established the imperial cult of emperor worship as a test of one's loyalty to the empire. Temples, altars, and statues to the emperors were built throughout the empire, and the people were required to sacrifice to the emperor.

Because the believers would not worship the emperor, they were persecuted. The Roman Emperor Domitian built an imperial cult center in Ephesus which included an altar and statue of Domitian. The local residents were required to bow down to and offer sacrifices to the image.

Domitian insisted on being called "the lord god" and issued coins bearing his image and this phrase. Naturally, this created a crisis for the believers in Ephesus. Could they "fix their sandals" in front of the statue as a way of bowing down to the image? Jewish and Christians leaders said, "No, we cannot pretend to worship the beast even though we really don't mean it." To refuse to bow down to the emperor meant persecution, exile, or death. The believers needed some assurance that God knew of their situation and had not forsaken them. This is the background to the Revelation.

SUGGESTED OUTLINE OF THE BOOK OF REVELATION

We begin our study with a survey of the Book of Revelation. The survey helps us see the "big picture" of the book so that we don't later get bogged down in the details. The following is an outline of the Book of Revelation that we will use in this three-volume series.

SUGGESTED OUTLINE OF THE BOOK OF REVELATION

HS = Heavenly Scene

ES = Earthly Scene

Chapter and Subject

1   The Revelation of Jesus in Glory (HS)

2-3   Letters to the Congregations (ES)

* Consecutive Sequence of Events—Other Chapters are Informational

Chapter 1 The Revelation of Jesus in Glory

1. Introduction and Blessing (verses 1-3)

In these introductory verses, John states right at the beginning that the purpose of this writing is to reveal the person of Jesus the Messiah. John boldly declares that God gave him this revelation through an angel.

As stated in Chapter 1, the word Revelation is translated from the Greek word *apokalypsis,* which means a disclosure or unveiling of something previously hidden. It is the Revelation of Jesus the Messiah.

The purpose of the Revelation is not only to glorify Jesus but also to show God's people things which would shortly come to pass. The Greek word translated as *shortly* can also mean quickly or swiftly and not necessarily imminent. John reassures his readers that he is writing everything he saw in a spiritual revelation. John promises a blessing to those who read, hear, and keep the words of the prophecy. He says the time is near, which suggests urgency to the reader.

2. Greeting to the Seven Congregations (verses 4-8)

Next John sends his greeting to the seven congregations. These congregations are located in the Roman Province of Asia Minor, which is modern-day Western Turkey. In light of their situation with the imperial cult, Jesus commends them, rebukes them, instructs them, and promises them a blessing if they remain faithful. John's greeting of grace and peace is in the name of the Father, the Son, and the Holy Spirit with an emphasis on Jesus as the Redeemer, Prophet, Priest, and King, whose coming to the earth will be witnessed by the whole world.

3. Vision of the Son of Man (verses 9-20)

John states his situation as being exiled to Patmos for the Word of God and for his testimony to Jesus. Then, in apocalyptic style, he claims a spiritual experience in which the Lord spoke to him to write a letter to the seven congregations. His vision of the Lord was the Son of Man. John uses symbols the people would understand in describing the Son of Man as Jesus standing in the midst of the seven churches (golden lampstands), dressed in His high priestly garments.

John further uses symbols to describe Jesus in His blazing glory and dazzling beauty. This vision so overwhelmed John that he fell to the ground. Jesus comforts John and declares His Lordship over life and death. Jesus instructs John to write the Revelation.

Chapter 2 Letters to the Congregations

1. Letter to Ephesus (verses 1-7)

The Lord had some good things to say to the congregation at Ephesus. They were firm in their beliefs and were busy "going about the Lord's work." However, they had lost their first love for the Lord. The situation at Ephesus represents a congregation that is very orthodox in their beliefs and doctrines and has many religious programs, but religion has replaced their relationship with the Lord. The Lord tells them to return to their first love. Certainly this would be a relevant word for God's people today. We are great at debating doctrine, but not as great at showing unconditional love.

2. Letter to Smyrna (verses 8-11)

Smyrna was a poor, persecuted congregation. The Lord speaks to them as One who was also poor and persecuted but overcame death. He has no rebuke for them, but reminds them that they are rich in spiritual things. He encourages them to be faithful in their times of testing, because their rewards will be great in the afterlife. They will overcome. Smyrna represents the persecuted congregation which always grows spiritually and numerically in difficult times. Today, millions of true believers around the world are suffering for their faith.

3. Letter to Pergamos (verses 12-17)

As mentioned earlier, Pergamos was a center of emperor worship. In addition, there were major shrines to other pagan deities. While the believers were steadfast in their beliefs because they were constantly faced with so much idol worship, they compromised some of their beliefs to accommodate their situation. The Lord tells them to repent.

Pergamos represents the congregation that is willing to compromise with and accommodate the world.

4.   Letter to Thyatira (verses 18-29)

The Lord commended the congregation at Thyatira, but He also rebuked them because they had allowed false teachers to come into their midst. The false teachers were leading the people astray by teaching them that certain practices were acceptable. The teachings had corrupted the people's morals. They were becoming a worldly congregation. The Lord encourages them to be faithful because they will overcome and rule with Him over the nations. Thyatira represents the worldly congregation.

Chapter 3 Letters to the Congregations

1.   Letter to Sardis (verses 1-6)

Unfortunately, the Lord did not have any good thing to say to the congregation at Sardis. While there were a few believers who remained faithful, the congregation as a whole was spiritually dead. They had religion without God. The Lord promised blessings to those who overcome, but called the congregation to repent. Sardis represents dead religious congregations that are Christian in name only.

2.   Letter to Philadelphia (verses 7-13)

The congregation in Philadelphia was faithfully persevering in a difficult area. While they were a small, seemingly insignificant congregation with little influence, they had remained faithful to the Lord and had not denied His name or His Word. As a result, the Lord did not rebuke this congregation. In view of their faithfulness, the Lord promised to be faithful to them by protecting them and delivering them from the evil one in their times of trials and tribulations. Philadelphia represents those many small congregations that don't have much influence and don't receive acclaim, but are faithful to the Lord.

3.   Letter to Laodicea (verses 14-22)

Nobody wants to be in a Laodicean congregation. The Lord calls them "lukewarm." The congregation in Laodicea was wealthy in material things but spiritually poor. Their wealth, comfort, and ease blinded them to spiritual things. They were an indifferent group content with "having church," but had no real commitment to the Lord or His Word. They were halfhearted, in-name-only believers who were self-sufficient and really didn't need nor want the Lord. They had Christianity "without Christ." The Lord gives a stern rebuke and calls them to repent, else He will spit them out like people spit out lukewarm water. Obviously, Laodicea represents today's rich congregations who are self-sufficient, indifferent, and blinded to spiritual things.

Chapter 4 The Throne Room of God in Heaven

1.   An Open Door to Heaven (verse 1)

In this chapter, John uses apocalyptic language to describe a prophetic vision of Heaven and the very throne room of God. In his spiritual state, John sees the throne room of God in all its glory and beauty, and all of Heaven worshiping God.

Scholars who believe in a dispensational interpretation of the Revelation see this as the rapture of the believers. In this view, John represents believers taken to Heaven during the tribulation until Revelation 19, at which time believers return to Earth to rule with the Lord. This teaching has a different plan for Israel and Christians. While the believers are in Heaven, the Jews are on Earth facing the wrath of the anti-Messiah and the nations.

However the Lord has this worked out, John's language is simply apocalyptic language to explain his spiritual experience. John wasn't literally caught up to Heaven. He didn't go anywhere. The readers of his time would have understood his intent. They would never have thought his words meant anything other than a spiritual vision.

2. The Throne Set in Heaven (verse 2-11)

In his spiritual vision, John sees the throne room of God which he describes in terms of precious stones. Around the throne, he sees four living creatures or beings, and 24 elders dressed in white and wearing crowns of gold. The four living beings and the 24 elders give constant worship to God.

Chapter 5 The Lamb on the Throne

1. The Lamb and the Scroll (verses 1-7)

In his heavenly spiritual state, John sees God holding a seven-sealed scroll. John weeps because no one is able to open the scroll. But one of the elders comforts John and identifies One who can open the scroll. This worthy One is the Lion of Judah, the Root of David. When John looks to see this Lion of Judah, he sees the Lamb of God, Jesus the resurrected worthy One, who is also the Lion of the Tribe of Judah.

2. Worthy Is the Lamb (verses 8-14)

When the Lamb takes the scroll, all of Heaven and all of the redeemed fall on their face and worship the Lamb. He is worthy to take the scroll because He has redeemed His people, who will reign with Him as kings and priests on the earth. This will have its ultimate fulfillment in the Messianic Kingdom when the Lord returns as described in Revelation 20. May His name be praised forever! Amen!

Chapter 6 Opening the First Six Seals

1. First Seal: The Conqueror (verses 1-2)

In the first seal, John sees a rider on a white horse going out to conquer.

2. Second Seal: War on the Earth (verses 3-4)

In the second seal, John sees a rider on a red horse causing war on the earth.

3.   Third Seal: Famine on the Earth (verses 5-6)

In the third seal, John sees a rider on a black horse causing famine on the earth.

4.   Fourth Seal: Disease and Death (verses 7-8)

In the fourth seal, John sees a rider on a pale horse causing death to one-fourth of the population on the earth.

5.   Fifth Seal: Cry of the Martyrs (verses 9-11)

In the fifth seal, John sees a multitude of tribulation martyrs crying out to the Lord to judge the evil on the earth and avenge their deaths.

6.   Sixth Seal: Cosmic Changes (verses 12-17)

In the sixth seal, John sees enormous changes taking place in Heaven which cause great upheaval on the earth. This is an apocalyptic way of saying that God is now pouring out His wrath on the earth with such power and force that all Heaven and Earth is being shaken.

Since this is apocalyptic symbolism, we may or may not interpret these events in a literal way. Regardless of how we should interpret what John describes, he wants us to realize that God's wrath is about to be manifested in Heaven and on Earth.

Chapter 7   God's Seal of Protection/Multitude of the Redeemed

1.   God's Seal of Protection (verses 1-8)

Before opening the seventh seal, the servants of God are sealed for protection. John lists 12,000 from each of the 12 tribes of Israel. Some see this as a representative number of all of God's servants, while the dispensational view see this as 144,000 Jews only.

2. Multitude of the Redeemed (verses 9-17)

John sees a great host of people worshiping the Lord. In reading the text, we are told that these are tribulation martyrs. Their suffering is not in vain, as John sees them overcoming and in the presence of the Living God and the Lamb.

Chapter 8 Opening the Seventh Seal: Trumpets-Shofars 1-4

1. Prelude to Opening the Seventh Seal (verses 1-6)

Before opening the seventh seal, there is a pause to show that now the prayers of the saints for the final judgment of God are to be answered.

2. First Trumpet-Shofar: Judgment on Vegetation (verses 7)

[A third of the trees and all grass are burned.]

3. Second Trumpet-Shofar: Judgment on the Sea (verses 8-9)

[A third of the sea becomes blood, a third of sea life dies, and a third of the ships are destroyed.]

4. Third Trumpet-Shofar: Judgment on Fresh Water (verses 10-11)

[A third of the fresh water becomes poisoned.]

5. Fourth Trumpet-Shofar: Judgment on the Celestial Bodies (verses 12-13)

[A third of the celestial bodies are darkened.]

Chapter 9 Opening the Seventh Seal: Trumpets-Shofars 5-6

1. Fifth Trumpet-Shofar: Demonic Attacks (verses 1-12)

[Demons are released from the bottomless pit and torment unbelievers for five months.]

2. Sixth Trumpet-Shofar: Release of Four Demonic Beings
    Who Had Been Bound at the Euphrates (verses 13-21)

[Four powerful demonic beings are released from the Euphrates and kill a third of mankind. Those who survive still do not repent.]

Chapter 10 The Mighty Angel With the Little Book

Chapter 10 is an interruption in the sequence of events. It is for information purposes.

1. The Mighty Angel With the Little Book (verses 1-7)

A powerful angel has a little book open in his hand. It certainly represents the Word of God regarding what is about to take place. When the angel speaks, it is like the sound of seven thunders. The angel forbids John from writing what he hears, but tells him to instead seal up the words he hears.

2. John Eats the Little Book (verses 8-11)

John is told to take the little book out of the hands of the angel and eat it. It is sweet in his mouth but bitter when digested. This is the Word of God that John is now to speak.

Chapter 11 The Two Witnesses

1. The Two Witnesses (verses 1-6)

In chapter 11, John describes the ministry of two witnesses who prophecy for three and a half years. They perform mighty miracles and are protected by the Lord during the three and a half years.

2. The Two Witnesses Killed (verses 7-10)

At the end of their time of ministry, the Lord allows satan to kill the two witnesses in Jerusalem. The people celebrate their deaths and keep their bodies on display for three and a half days.

3. The Two Witnesses Resurrected (verses 11-14)

After the three and a half days, the Lord resurrects the two witnesses and takes them to Heaven. He then sends a judgment on the city in the form of an earthquake, killing 7,000 people.

4. The Seventh Trumpet-Shofar Proclaiming the Kingdom of God (verses 15-19)

Then the seventh angel sounds, proclaiming the Kingdom of God is ready to be revealed. As a side note, the story of the Book of Revelation actually ends here. The rest of the Book of Revelation gives the details of what actually happens like an instant replay of the events.

Chapter 12 War in Heaven and on Earth

1. The Woman, the Child, and the Dragon (verses 1-6)

John sees a heavenly scene of warfare between a woman, a child, and a dragon. The woman is most likely Israel and possibly the grafted-in believers, the Child is clearly the Messiah, and the dragon is satan. Satan convinces a third of the angels in Heaven to follow him in his attempt to destroy the Child at His birth. God protects the woman for three and a half years.

2. Satan Thrown out of Heaven (verses 7-12)

John continues to see the war in Heaven. Satan is cast out of Heaven to the earth where he seeks to destroy the works of God and the people of God. But God's people overcame satan by the blood of the Lamb and the word of their testimony.

3. The Woman Persecuted (verses 13-17)

John now sees the war on the earth as satan attempts to destroy the woman. However, God protects the woman from satan, who then turns his wrath against any of the people of God he can find.

Chapter 13 The Two False Messiahs

1. The Beast From the Sea (verses 1-10)

Using apocalyptic language, John sees two evil persons handpicked by the devil to make war against the saints. The first beast is said to come out of the sea, which usually means from the nations. This beast rules over the nations, empowered by satan. He makes war against the saints for three and one half years. Most of the world worships the beast, except for those whose names are written in the Book of Life, and perhaps others who have not yet embraced the Messiah.

2. The Beast From the Earth (verses 11-18)

John then sees another beast which he describes as coming from the earth. Whereas the beast from the sea is the political leader of the world, this beast is the False Prophet who, by signs and wonders, deceives people into worshiping the first beast. He convinces most of the world to take the mark of the beast in order to conduct business.

Chapter 14 Preview of the End

This is a preview of things to come and does not advance the narrative of the story.

1. The Lamb and the 144,000 (verses 1-5)

John sees the 144,000 in the presence of the Lamb of God. They sing a new song of the redeemed to the Lord. They are described as pure before the Lord.

2. The Proclamation of Three Angels (verses 6-13)

John sees three angels making three different proclamations. The first angel proclaims the Gospel of the Kingdom to all the people on the earth. The second angel proclaims judgment on Babylon (Rome and the world system), and the third angel proclaims judgment on all who have worshiped the Beast and received his mark.

3. Reaping the Earth's Harvest (verses 14-16)

This is the first of two harvest reapings. The first harvest seems to be believers being separated from the next harvest of unbelievers. This would be the rapture of believers.

4. Reaping the Grapes of Wrath (verses 17-20)

This is a continuation of the previous harvest. It seems to be God's final judgment and complete destruction of the ungodly.

Chapter 15 Preparing for the Seventh Trumpet-Shofar

In this chapter, John sees Heaven preparing for the sounding of the seventh trumpet-shofar, which will unleash the seven bowl judgments on the earth.

Chapter 16 Sounding the Seventh Trumpet-Shofar (Seven Bowl Judgments)

1. First Bowl Judgment: Loathsome Sores (verses 1-2)

2. Second Bowl Judgment: The Sea Turns to Blood (verse 3)

3. Third Bowl Judgment: The Waters Turn to Blood (verses 4-7)

4. Fourth Bowl Judgment: The Scorching Sun (verses 8-9)

5. Fifth Bowl Judgment: Darkness and Pain (verses 10-11)

6. Sixth Bowl Judgment: Euphrates Dries Up (verses 12-16)

7. Seventh Bowl Judgment: The Earth Is Shaken (verses 17-21)

Chapter 17 Destruction of World Religious System

1. The Great Harlot and the Beast (verses 1-6)

An angel shows John the great harlot and the beast in all their majesty, drunk with the blood of God's people.

2. The Meaning of the Great Harlot and the Beast (verses 7-18)

An angel explains to John the mystery of the harlot and the beast. The harlot symbolizes the false one-world religious system, and the beast symbolizes the one-world political system.

Chapter 18 Destruction of World Political System

An angel shows John God's judgment and complete destruction of Babylon—the anti-God world political system.

1. Announcing the Fall of Babylon (verses 1-8)

2. The World Mourns Babylon's Fall (verses 9-20)

3. God's Final Judgment on Babylon (verses 21-24)

Chapter 19 Second Coming of Messiah

In this chapter, John hears all of Heaven celebrating God's judgment of Babylon—the world system; and the coming of the Lord to judge and make war against the Beast, the False Prophet, and the nations who gave their allegiance to the Beast.

1. Heaven Celebrates the Fall of Babylon (verses 1-10)

2. The Coming of the Lord (verses 11-16)

3. The Lord Defeats the Beast and His Armies (verses 17-21)

Chapter 20 Thousand-Year Messianic Kingdom

John sees an angel binding satan, the Lord's reign with His saints for 1,000 years, the loosing and rebellion of satan, and the Great White Throne Judgment.

1. Satan Bound for a Thousand Years (verses 1-3)

2. The Thousand-Year Messianic Kingdom (verses 4-6)

3. Satan's Rebellion (verses 7-10)

4. The Great White Throne Judgment (verses 11-15)

Chapter 21 New Heaven and New (Restored) Earth

In Chapters 21-22, John sees the New Heaven and the New Earth. The New Jerusalem descends to the earth and is the final home and destiny of all of God's people of all time. Time ends and eternity begins.

1. The New Heaven and the New (Restored) Earth (verses 1-8)

2. The New Jerusalem (verses 9-21)

3. The Glory of the New Jerusalem (verses 22-27)

Chapter 22 Paradise Restored

1. The River of Life (verses 1-5)

2. Confirming the Revelation to John (verses 6-11)

3. Confirming the Revelation to the Congregations (verses 12-17)

4. Warning Not to Change the Prophecy (verses 18-19)

5. Assurance of the Prophecy (verses 20-21)

REVIEW QUESTIONS

1. Write a summary of what you have learned in this lesson. Write the summary in clear concise words as if you are going to present it to another person.

2. Write an explanation of how you can apply what you have learned in this lesson to your life.

3. Share what you have learned with your family, friends, and members of your study group.

Chapter 4

The Revelation of Jesus in Glory—
Part One

REVELATION REVIEW

B ECAUSE the Book of Revelation is apocalyptic literature filled
with symbols, we often lose focus of the purpose of this book
and spend too much time trying to understand the meaning of
the symbols. While it is good to understand as much as we can about
the symbols, the Book of Revelation is not about the symbols. It is not
about the anti-Messiah, the Mark of the Beast, the False Prophet, the
rapture, the tribulation, etc. While these are certainly important subjects, they are not the focus of the book.

John tells us up front that this is the Revelation of Jesus Christ
(Yeshua the Messiah). So the purpose and focus of our study of the
Book of Revelation should be the Lord Himself and not the symbols.
We can have different interpretations about the symbols and debate
what they mean, but this only causes division and does not help us in
our walk with God. We should spend our time and energy preparing
for His coming rather than arguing about things we don't understand.

After giving his opening comment and blessing, John sends his greeting to the seven congregations. As we learned in the introductory chapter and repeat here, these are seven literal congregations located in the Western Roman province of Asia Minor, which is modern-day Turkey. They were all experiencing a measure of persecution because of the emperor worship which Domitian had enforced in the late '90s of the first century. The Lord had a word for each of these congregations which He is sending them through John. Let's join John now as he tells us about his remarkable vision.

INTRODUCTION AND GREETING TO THE SEVEN CONGREGATIONS (REVELATION 1:1-8)

The purpose of this first chapter in John's revelation is to reveal the glory of Jesus in Heaven. We can divide the chapter into three parts: 1) the introduction and blessing, 2) the greeting to the seven congregations, and 3) the vision of the Son of Man. We will study the first two parts in this chapter.

INTRODUCTION AND BLESSING (VERSES 1-3)

We learned in Chapter 1 that the Greek word for *apocalypse* means revelation, disclosure or unveiling. This book is the revelation, the disclosure, the unveiling of Jesus the Son of Man and Son of God, the Messiah who is the Lion of the Tribe of Judah coming to judge the nations and establish His literal Kingdom on the earth.

The Hebrew Scriptures speak of a personal deliverer who would be sent by God for the purpose of ruling Israel and the nations with justice and righteousness. He would usher in the golden age of peace and prosperity about which the prophets spoke.

It was the Lord's desire that the Jewish people be able to recognize the Messiah when He came on the scene. As a result, God gave many details about the Messiah to the prophets who passed this information on to the people. These prophecies provided the necessary details about the birth, life, death, and rule of the Messiah to enable the Jewish people to recognize Him.

However, as the Jewish sages studied these prophecies, they became confused over what seemed to be a contradiction. There were some prophecies that spoke about the Messiah as being a great King and Deliverer who would destroy the enemies of Israel and establish her as the head nation of the earth. In this role, the Messiah would be a great political-military Messiah.

On the other hand, there were other prophecies that spoke of the Messiah as being a humble and gentle teacher who would suffer greatly and be put to death, bearing the sins of the people and making atonement for them before God. These prophecies described a religious Messiah.

The two portraits of the Messiah were very clear. What was not clear was how both could be speaking about the same person. The greatest of scholars could not harmonize these two seemingly contradictory portraits of the Messiah.

Some scholars thought that perhaps two Messiahs would come. One Messiah would be the political-military ruler, while the other would be the religious ruler. The political-military Messiah would establish the kingdom of David and bring to pass the nationalistic promises of the Abrahamic covenant. The religious leader would establish the Kingdom of God and put into effect the spiritual promises of the Abrahamic covenant.

This is exactly what the anti-Messiah and False Prophet will attempt to accomplish during the tribulation period. Unfortunately, some number of Jews and much of the world will be deceived by their trickery.

For centuries, the Jewish people have looked for the coming of the Messiah. As time passed, they found themselves subjected to one

Gentile power after another: Assyria, Babylon, Medo-Persia, Greece, and finally Rome.

The Jews longed to be free from foreign domination. They naturally focused their attention on the prophecies that spoke about the Messiah as the Great Deliverer. They wanted a political-military Messiah who would overthrow the Romans and restore the sovereignty of Israel as a nation. I certainly understand that longing.

In their desperation, the Jewish people naturally tended to ignore the prophecies that spoke of the Messiah as a religious leader. They had enough of suffering, persecution, and death. The rabbis downplayed this role of the Messiah. They told the people what they wanted to hear like many Christian ministers do today. After a time, generations of young Jews only knew the political-military portrait of the Messiah. They had Messianic tunnel vision. They could only see this one view of Messiah. This was the situation during the time of Jesus of Nazareth.

What the sages were not able to understand was that both portraits of the Messiah would be fulfilled in one person, but not at the same time. There would be a time gap between the two roles the Messiah would play. This would require Him to appear on the earth at two different times.

The first time, the Messiah would come as the religious Messiah to bring atonement for sin and to establish the spiritual realm of the Kingdom of God in the hearts of mankind. He would come as the Lamb of God to take away the sins of the world. Then, after a period of time, He would come again as the political-military Messiah to establish the physical Kingdom of God over all the earth and the physical kingdom of David to Israel. This is the subject of the Book of Revelation.

Isaiah explains:

> Now it shall come to pass in the latter days that the mountain of the LORD's house shall be established on the top of the mountains, and shall be exalted above the hills; and

all nations shall flow to it. Many people shall come and say, "Come, let us go up to the mountain of the LORD, to the house of the God of Jacob; He will teach us His ways, and we shall walk in His paths." For out of Zion shall go forth the law, and the word of the LORD from Jerusalem. He shall judge between the nations, and rebuke many people; they shall beat their swords into plowshares, and their spears into pruning hooks; nation shall not lift up sword against nation, neither shall they learn war anymore (Isaiah 2:2-4).

Isaiah further says:

Of the increase of His government and peace there will be no end, upon the throne of David and over His kingdom, to order it and to establish it with judgment and justice from that time forward, even forever. The zeal of the Lord of hosts will perform this (Isaiah 9:7).

Our Father in Heaven gave Jesus this revelation to give to John through an angel. Revelation 22:16 says, *"I, Jesus, have sent My angel to testify to you these thing in the churches* [Congregations]. *I am the Root and the Offspring of David, the Bright and Morning Star."* Angels are very active in the Book of Revelation, being mentioned 67 times.

God often uses angels to carry out His work on the earth. They deliver messages (see Luke 1:26-28), protect the people of God (see Dan. 6:22), give guidance (see Exod. 14:19), offer encouragement (see Gen. 16:7), bring punishment (see 2 Sam. 24:16), patrol the earth (see Ezek.1:9-14), fight the forces of evil (see Dan. 10:12-13), interpret dreams and visions (see Dan. 8:16), offer praise to God (see Rev. 19:1-3), and perform any other service for which God might want them.

It is interesting that God used angels to announce the first coming of Jesus in Luke 1:8-14 and will use them again to announce His second coming in Revelation 11:15. In these Scriptures we learn that angels were the first beings to actually preach the Gospel.

The purpose of giving this Revelation is so that we can know the future. Nonbelievers spend a lot of time and money trying to know the future. But God is the only One who knows the future, because He transcends time. This means that He has already lived the future.

Isaiah explains:

> *Remember the former things of old, for I am God, and there is no other; I am God, and there is none like Me, declaring the end from the beginning, and from ancient times things that are not yet done, saying, "My counsel shall stand, and I will do all My pleasure"* (Isaiah 46:9-10).

John says that he is writing about things which must shortly take place. Since God is outside of time, in His mind, the future is now or imminent. Peter wrote:

> *But, beloved, do not forget this one thing, that with the Lord one day is as a thousand years, and a thousand years as one day. The Lord is not slack concerning His promise, as some count slackness, but is longsuffering toward us, not willing that any should perish but that all should come to repentance* (2 Peter 3:8-9).

The idea is that whenever God puts these events into motion, they will happen quickly. People will not have time to get prepared because the events will unfold too fast. So God's people had better already be prepared. As I shared earlier, some of these events took place in John's time, while others will happen at the end of the age before the return of Jesus. As we see the signs of the times, we certainly seem to be living in the latter days.

John testifies that he saw all the things which he recorded and revealed about Jesus. As a result, he pronounces a blessing on those who take heed to his words. In fact, there is a sevenfold blessing in the Book of Revelation.

SEVENFOLD BLESSING

1. God blesses those who read, hear and obey the prophecy.

    Blessed is he who reads and those who hear the words of this prophecy, and keep those things which are written in it; for the time is near (Revelation 1:3).

2. God blesses those who die in the Lord.

    Then I heard a voice from heaven saying to me, "Write: Blessed are the dead who die in the Lord from now on." "Yes," says the Spirit, "that they may rest from their labors, and their works follow them" (Revelation 14:13).

3. God blesses the watchman.

    Behold, I am coming as a thief. Blessed is he who watches, and keeps his garments, lest he walk naked and they see his shame (Revelation 16:15).

4. God blesses those who are invited to the wedding feast of the Lamb.

    Then he said to me, "Write: 'Blessed are those who are called to the marriage supper of the Lamb!'" And he said to me, "These are the true sayings of God" (Revelation 19:9).

5. God blesses those who share in the first resurrection.

   Blessed and holy is he who has part in the first resurrection. Over such the second death has no power, but they shall be priests of God and of Christ [Messiah], *and shall reign with Him for a thousand years* (Revelation 20:6).

6. God blesses those who obey the prophecy in the Book of Revelation.

   Behold, I am coming quickly! Blessed is he who keeps the words of the prophecy of this book (Revelation 22:7).

7. God blesses those who do His commandments.

   Blessed are those who do His commandments [wash their robes], *that they may have the right to the tree of life, and may enter through the gates into the city* (Revelation 22:14).

GREETINGS TO THE SEVEN CONGREGATIONS
(VERSES 4-8)

After giving his opening comment and blessing, John gives his greeting to the seven congregations. As we learned earlier, these are seven literal congregations located in the Western Roman province of Asia Minor, which is modern-day Turkey. They were all experiencing a measure of persecution because of the emperor worship which Domitian had enforced in the late '90s of the first century.

In the Bible, the number seven often represents completion. So even though there were other local congregations in the area, these seven were representative of the others. John may have chosen to write to these particular congregations because they were conveniently located on the main Roman road in the area. The letter most likely was circulated clockwise beginning at Ephesus and then to Smyrna, Pergamos, Thyatira, Sardis, Philadelphia, and finally to Laodicea.

John begins with the words *grace* and *peace* which was a standard greeting in his day. Paul used the same greeting in his letters. John was extending to them the grace and peace of God and from God, which they definitely needed considering their difficult circumstances.

In fact, John includes in his greeting the Father, the Son, and the Holy Spirit. He references the Father by the phrase, *"who is and who was and who is to come"* (Rev. 1:8). This wording takes us back to Exodus 3:14 when the One True God called Moses to confront Pharaoh and lead the people out of Egypt.

In Bible times, deities were known by their names. This is because the name told about the nature and character of the deity. Moses wanted to know which God was speaking to him, and in whose name he was going to speak to Pharaoh. God said to Moses, *"I AM WHO I AM."*

God's name means "He is who He will be." Technically, it means that He is the self-existing, uncaused One who transcends time and space. He is who He will be forever in time and space. He is all-sufficient for whatever He needs to be and for whatever we need Him to be. He is the "I AM." John greets the congregations with grace and peace from the "I AM."

Now if that is not enough to encourage them, John also includes the Holy Spirit in his greeting. He refers to the Holy Spirit as the *"seven Spirits who are before His* [God's] *throne"* (Rev. 1:4). Once again, seven is the number of completion or fullness. In this instance, it refers to the perfect Holy Spirit who receives God's Words and gives them to God's people.

Jesus said in John 16:13 that when the Spirit comes, *"He will guide you into all truth, for He will not speak on His own authority, but whatever*

He hears, He will speak; and He will tell you the things to come." We also see a similar reference to the Holy Spirit in Isaiah 11:2.

JESUS—PROPHET, PRIEST, AND KING

Now if that is not enough to encourage them, John also includes a greeting from Jesus. He calls Jesus *"the faithful witness, the firstborn from the dead, and the ruler* [or prince] *over the kings of the earth"* (Rev. 1:5). By referring to Jesus in this way, John is acknowledging that Jesus is Messiah who functions as the perfect Prophet, the perfect High Priest, and the perfect King of kings and Lord of lords.

In Bible times, when a prophet, priest, or king began his ministry, he was anointed with oil to set him apart for his work. As such, prophets, priests, and kings were considered a type of a Messiah or anointed one because they spoke God's Words, interceded with God for the people, and ruled over the people.

Moses is considered the greatest of all the prophets, but He failed. He disobeyed God. God told Moses to speak to the rock, but instead, Moses struck the rock. That little act of disobedience cost Moses the Promised Land. He got to look over, but didn't get to go into the Land.

Aaron is considered the greatest of all the High Priests, but he also failed. When Moses was on the mountaintop seeking God, Aaron was down below making a golden calf for the people to worship. When Moses confronted Him, Aaron made an excuse. He said he just threw the gold into the fire and out came a calf.

David is considered the greatest of all the kings, but he too failed. In his lust for Bathsheba, he had her husband killed and then took her as his wife. God was displeased and took the life of their first child. David was forgiven, but suffered the consequences for his sin the rest of his life.

Now, surely, God must have someone waiting in the wings who is greater than Moses, greater than Aaron, and greater than David. Surely there must be a perfect prophet, a perfect priest, and a perfect king. Yes, there is One greater.

Moses spoke of a prophet who would come after him. Deuteronomy reads:

> *I will raise up for them a Prophet like you from among their brethren, and will put My words in His mouth, and He shall speak to them all that I command Him. And it shall be that whoever will not hear My words, which He speaks in My name, I will require it of him* (Deuteronomy 18:18-19).

Every time God would raise up a new prophet, the people would wonder, "Is this the prophet?" They were waiting for that One greater than Moses. But time went by and none proved worthy.

God told King David that he would have a son who would sit on David's throne forever. David's house, David's kingdom, and David's throne would be established forever (see 2 Sam. 7:16). Every time God would raise up a new king, the people would wonder, "Is this the Greater Son of David?" But time went by and none proved worthy.

God appointed Aaron and his family to be the priestly clan. The priesthood had to be passed to the next generation. But they all died. They all made mistakes. Time went by and none proved worthy.

When Jesus began His ministry, He asked His *talmidim* (disciples):

> ... *"Who do men say that I, the Son of Man, am?" So they said, "Some say John the Baptist, some Elijah, and others Jeremiah or one of the prophets." He said to them, "But who do you say that I am?" Simon Peter answered and said, "You are the Christ, the Son of the living God."*

*Jesus answered and said to him, "Blessed are you, Simon
Bar-Jonah, for flesh and blood has not revealed this to
you, but My Father who is in heaven. And I also say to
you that you are Peter, and on this rock* [this confession]
I will build My church [congregation], *and the gates of
Hades shall not prevail against it"* (Matthew 16:13-18).

Peter was acknowledging that Jesus was the Messiah. He was the
prophet greater than Moses. He was the priest greater than Aaron, and
He was the king greater than David. Or as John said, *"He is the faithful
witness, the firstborn from the dead, and the ruler* [or prince] *over the
kings of the earth."*

When Jesus came the first time, He came in the role of the Prophet—
the Word of God in human flesh. Jesus is presently interceding for us in
Heaven as our great High Priest who ever lives to make intercession for
us. He is returning as King of kings and Lord of lords.

The Roman emperor is not the Lord God. The God of Abraham,
Isaac, and Jacob is the Lord God. And His Son Jesus is the Messiah.
When John finished writing these words, he was not able to hold back
his praise. He said:

*To Him who loved us and washed us from our sins in His
own blood, and has made us kings and priests to His God
and Father, to Him be glory and dominion forever and
ever. Amen* (Revelation 1:5-6).

God loves us and sent His only uniquely born Son to die for our sins
so that we can be forgiven and have fellowship with the Father. So that
we can serve God and people as His priests, and so that we can rule and
reign with Him on the earth.

And one day, in God's own time, He is going to return to judge the
nations and establish His Messianic Kingdom on the earth. His coming
will be personal and visible to the whole world. Every eye will see Him,

including His Jewish brethren who rejected Him. All will mourn when they realize the One they have been waiting for is none other than Jesus of Nazareth.

Zechariah says:

> *And I will pour on the house of David and on the inhabitants of Jerusalem the Spirit of grace and supplication; then they will look on Me whom they pierced. Yes, they will mourn for Him as one mourns for his only son, and grieve for Him as one grieves for a firstborn* (Zechariah 12:10).

Jesus said:

> *...Then the sign of the Son of Man will appear in heaven, and then all the tribes of the earth will mourn, and they will see the Son of Man coming on the clouds of heaven with power and great glory* (Matthew 24:30).

When Jesus ascended to Heaven from the Mount of Olives, two angels appeared to the people as they stared into the sky and said:

> *Men of Galilee, why do you stand gazing up into heaven? This same Jesus, who was taken up from you into heaven, will so come in like manner as you saw Him go into heaven* (Acts 1:11).

Now, just to make sure everyone understands that God is in charge, He finishes up where John left off, and says, "*I am the Alpha and the Omega, the Beginning and the End,' says the Lord, 'who is and who was and who is to come, the Almighty*'" (Rev. 1:8).

REVIEW QUESTIONS

1. Write a summary of what you have learned in this lesson. Write the summary in clear concise words as if you are going to present it to another person.

2. Write an explanation of how you can apply what you have learned in this lesson to your life.

3. Share what you have learned with your family, friends, and members of your study group.

Chapter 5

The Revelation of Jesus in Glory— Part Two

REVELATION REVIEW

JOHN introduces his writing as the Revelation of Jesus Christ (Yeshua the Messiah). This tells us what his vision and disclosure is about. It is about Jesus. It is not about the anti-Messiah, the Mark of the Beast, the meaning of 666, the False Prophet, or the New World Order. These subjects are part of his vision and certainly important, but they are neither the purpose nor the focus of the Book of Revelation.

For some reason, it is human nature to spend our time studying and arguing about that which is less important. Perhaps this is because the above-mentioned subjects are somewhat sensational, and people love to talk about sensational subjects. While it is important to know about these lesser subjects, it is more important to know what John says about Jesus. As believers, there is no subject more sensational and exciting than Jesus Himself. I urge you to keep your focus on Jesus as you read this three-volume series.

John explains that the Lord gave him this message through an angel and that through his writing, John is bearing witness to what the angel showed him. John promises seven blessings to those who will read, hear, and keep or do the words written in the prophecy. He especially mentions those who *hear* the words of the prophecy, because scholars tell us that less than 20 percent of the people of that time could read.

It is important to note that the blessing promises required the readers and hearers to actually obey the Lord's instructions. The promise to the overcomer was, and still is, only to those who obey. This is so very important for Western Christians who "hear but don't do." Knowing God's Word is not the same as doing God's Word. In fact, if we know God's Word but don't obey it, we would be better off if we had not known it. This is because God holds us accountable for the light He gives us. As we begin our study of this incredible vision, I encourage you to be an overcomer by obeying what the Lord shows you.

After introducing his vision, John greets the seven congregations with a message of grace and peace from our heavenly Father, the Holy Spirit and Jesus. He refers to Jesus as the Prophet, the Priest and the King of the universe. Recall that in Bible times, when a prophet, a priest, or a king began his ministry, he was anointed with oil. They were considered a type of Messiah *(Mashiach)* or anointed one because they spoke God's Word, interceded for the people, and ruled over the people. While they all failed in one way or another, Jesus is the perfect Prophet, the perfect High Priest, and the perfect King. In other words, Jesus is the Messiah.

Because of His great love, Jesus has redeemed us by the shedding of His own blood. He has made us His kings and priests on the earth, and He is returning to establish His Kingdom on the earth, at which time we will rule and reign with Him over the nations. Hallelujah!

VISION OF THE SON OF MAN
(REVELATION CHAPTER 1:9-20)

Now that John has properly greeted the people, he shares his exciting vision of the Son of Man. He sees Jesus as a Jewish Messiah, not as a Western Christian. This is why it is so important for Christians to understand the Hebraic roots of our faith.

IDENTIFYING WITH HIS READERS (VERSE 9)

In apocalyptic literature, it was common for the writer to put someone else's name on his writing. This was usually a famous person, naturally deceased, to whom the writer wanted to attribute his ideas. Of course we would not do this today but it was common in ancient times among Jews, Christians, and pagans. This type of writing was called *pseudepigrapha*, which is a Greek word meaning "falsely inscribed or attributed."

There was a large body of Jewish *pseudepigrapha* written between 200 B.C. and A.D. 200. The writer, who was anonymous, attributed his work to one of the ancient patriarchs or prophets. In the work, the writer attempted to record his own ideas as if they were the ideas and writings of a well-known biblical character written in an apocalyptic manner. These works include the Apocalypse of Abraham, the Apocalypse of Adam, the books of Adam and Eve, the book of Enoch, the book of the Secrets of Enoch, the Testament of Moses, the Testament of the Twelve Patriarchs, and many others. There were also a number of New Testament *pseudepigrapha* written in the time when John received his revelation. These were spurious works attributed to New Testament personalities, such as the Gospel of Thomas, the Gospel of Barnabas, the Gospel of Judas, the Gospel of Phillip, the Gospel of Mary, the Gospel of Peter, the Epistle of Clement, etc. When it was decided which books were genuine and to be included in the New Testament, these books were rejected. The movie *The Da Vinci Code* was based on the *pseudepigrapha* of the Gospel of Thomas.

The point in providing this information is that John actually put his own name on his Revelation. His was not some spurious document where he was trying to convince his audience that some other biblical personality received this revelation. He received it himself from the Lord, as anyone could confirm, as he was still alive.

Without this background, we would not understand the significance of John mentioning his own name in verse one and again in verses four and nine. It was a real revelation received by a real, living person from the real, living Lord, for real people in John's time plus future generations. To John's readers, this was very important.

To more authenticate his writing, John even states where he was when he received his revelation. He was on the island of Patmos. Patmos is a small, rocky island about ten miles long and six miles wide located in the Aegean Sea about 40 miles from the coast of Turkey.

Similar to Alcatraz, the Romans used Patmos as an island prison for troublemakers and criminals. And John was considered a troublemaker because he preached the Word of God and said that Jesus, not Domitian, was Lord. It is amazing that evil rulers are so afraid of the Word of God and the testimony of Jesus. Today, Patmos has a population of approximately 50,000, including the massive monastery dedicated to John.

As explained in previous chapters, John is writing to believers who are suffering persecution for their faith. They would not bow to the statue of Domitian and acknowledge him as Lord and God. Christian tradition is that John had lived in Ephesus, from which he was exiled to Patmos. The Christian historian, Eusebius, wrote that John was exiled from Ephesus to Patmos in A.D. 95 and was released 18 months later.

Since John was persecuted along with the others, he was able to write that he was their brother and companion in the tribulation and Kingdom and patience of Jesus Christ [Yeshua the Messiah]. We note that John did not mention Christianity or "Churchianity." He mentioned the Kingdom of Jesus. The point is that the New Testament emphasis is not on the Gospel of salvation but on the Gospel of the Kingdom. John would certainly give this emphasis, because he was writing to people who were living under the rule of an emperor in an anti-God empire. They were Kingdom-minded.

Yes, God wants to save us from our sins. But much more than that, He desires to rule as Lord and King in our lives. If Domitian presents himself as lord and god, how much more does the One True God, Maker of Heaven and Earth, have rightful claim on our lives?

John the Baptist, Jesus and Paul, and now John emphasize the Gospel of the Kingdom, not the Gospel of salvation. In Christian terms, we would say that Jesus is not just our Savior, but He is also Lord of our lives. This has not been the Gospel emphasis in Western Christianity, but it is the emphasis in the Bible. One of the reasons why Christianity in America has not seen signs and wonders as the norm is because signs and wonders accompany the Gospel of the Kingdom, not the Gospel of salvation.

In Matthew 10:7-8, Jesus said to His followers:

> And as you go, preach, saying, "The kingdom of heaven is at hand." Heal the sick, cleanse the lepers, raise the dead, cast out demons, Freely you have received, freely give.

Matthew 9:35 says:

> Then Jesus went about all the cities and villages, teaching in their synagogues, preaching the gospel of the kingdom, and healing every sickness and every disease among the people.

In Matthew 24:14, Jesus gave one of the signs of the endtimes. He said:

> This gospel of the kingdom will be preached in all the world as a witness to the nations, and then the end will come.

So how did we go from the biblical presentation of the Gospel of the Kingdom to the Gospel of salvation? When anything in Christianity changed from the way it was in the Bible, we usually go back to Constantine.

When Constantine embraced Christianity as the official religion of the Roman Empire, he merged the political and the religious so that they were synonymous with the Roman Empire. The organized Church and the state were one and the same under the rule of Constantine.

Later, Augustine wrote that the Roman State-Church was the embodiment of the Kingdom of God on the earth. As a result, Europeans were born (at birth) into the Roman State-Church which was presented as the earthly manifestation of the Kingdom of God. Christian "Churchianity" in the form of the Roman State-Church replaced Israel, the Jews, and the Kingdom of God to the people. So their allegiance was to the Roman State-Church, not to the Kingdom of God.

In the Protestant Reformation in the 1500s, the organized Protestant churches replaced the Roman Catholic Church, and the idea of loyalty to the Protestant version of Christianity continued. The reformer replaced the Pope, and the particular reform group replaced the Catholic Church, which in turn had replaced the Kingdom of God.

The Protestant denominations have continued the concept of "Churchianity" to this day, but are becoming irrelevant to younger people who rightly see them as antiquated relics of the past. As an increasing number of young believers attend independent congregations, they will become more and more open and aware of Kingdom concepts and Kingdom living.

While we appreciate all of God's ministers who have faithfully proclaimed the Gospel of salvation throughout Christian history, the end-time Gospel will not be about "getting saved and joining the church." It will be the Gospel of the Kingdom. We see this model described in the Revelation:

Then the seventh angel sounded: And there were loud voices in heaven, saying, "The kingdoms of this world have become the kingdoms of our Lord and of His Christ [Messiah], and He shall reign forever and ever!" (Revelation 11:15).

As we awaken to this shift of emphasis from the Gospel of salvation to the Gospel of the Kingdom, from "Churchianity" to Kingdom life, we will see biblical kinds of miracles as common place for believers who are willing to submit themselves to Jesus as Lord. The greatest outpouring of God's supernatural manifestations is at hand. While evil will increase, the glory of God's Spirit will anoint His faithful people with His presence and His power as we see in the New Testament, because we will have a New Testament Gospel.

Human nature is such that it is difficult for us to have empathy and compassion with people who suffer unless we have shared in their suffering. This is not the case with John. He reminds them that he has shared and continues to share in their tribulation. That is why he was banished to Patmos in the first place.

From the very beginning of Christianity, believers have suffered for their faith. The degree of persecution against Christians was greater in the 20th century than in all other centuries combined. It is estimated that approximately 100 million believers died for their faith in the 20th century. Tens of thousands, if not hundreds of thousands, of believers are martyred every year in Africa, Asia, and the Middle East. I urge every believer to read *Fox's Book of Martyrs* to get an understanding of the price most martyrs have paid to follow Jesus.[1]

It is only in modern times that Christians in Western Europe, and particularly in America, have not been persecuted as government policy for their faith. Christians have not been persecuted overtly in America because America is the only nation that was birthed out of a Judeo-Christian heritage. America is the one exception in the history of nations. That is rapidly changing.

Already, Europe is post-Christian. Both Jews and true believers in Europe who speak out against Islam and who are considered politically incorrect are coming under intense persecution. As America more and more despises its Judeo-Christian heritage, anti-Semitic and anti-Christian voices will become more and more militant against Jews and Bible-believing Christians who stand for biblical morals. Bible-believing Christian voices will continue to be ridiculed and marginalized. Persecution always follows.

Suffering for the sake of righteousness is the norm, not the exception as it has been in America. American Christians who don't know history nor have a biblical worldview, and think our life of acceptance and ease is the norm, are going to be shocked into the reality of what it means to be a true believer in a hostile culture.

We may all have to decide if we are able to "fix our sandals" in front of the statute of the emperor. If faced with the choice, are we going to compromise our beliefs to be politically correct, to keep the local government enforcers away from our door and avoid persecution? Or will we be strong like the believers to whom John is writing? Our "easy-believism" Gospel of salvation will not be enough to help us stand against the forces of evil. We must embrace Jesus as Lord and King of our lives.

Jesus said, *"In this world you will have tribulation; but be of good cheer, I have overcome the world"* (John 16:33).

Paul wrote to his young disciple Timothy, *"all who desire to live godly in Christ Jesus will suffer persecution"* (2 Tim. 3:12).

Peter was soon to be martyred when he wrote:

> *But even if you should suffer for righteousness sake, you are blessed. And do not be afraid of their threats, nor be troubled. But sanctify the Lord God in your hearts, and always be ready to give a defense to everyone who asks*

you a reason for the hope that is in you, with meekness and fear (1 Peter 3:14-15).

Therefore let those who suffer according to the will of God commit their souls to Him in doing good, as to a faithful Creator (1 Peter 4:19).

THE APOCALYPTIC STATEMENT (VERSE 10)

Now that John has identified himself as the true writer of his revelation and one who is sharing in the fellowship of their suffering, he makes his apocalyptic statement. He says three things: 1) I was in the Spirit, 2) it was on the Lord's Day, and 3) I heard a loud voice like the sound of the trumpet or shofar.

By saying he was in the Spirit, the readers would understand that John was having a mystical apocalyptic vision. He was going to reveal to them things happening in Heaven which they could not see but which would explain what was happening to them on the earth. We cannot see the spiritual battles in Heaven, but we can have some knowledge of them by seeing them manifested on the earth. For example, we can know there is a great battle happening in Heaven for Jerusalem as we see the nations gather against Israel.

John gives four apocalyptic "in-the-Spirit" statements in the Revelation. These refer to his visions. (See Revelation 1:10; 4:2; 17:3; 21:10.) These statements provide the basic structure to the Book of Revelation.

John specifically says that he has this apocalyptic vision on the Lord's Day. Now, our Western Christian scholars will give us a footnote reference in our Bible that says something like, "This is referring to John worshiping the Lord on the first day of the week." That gives us the impression that John was having a nice little Sunday morning church service.

But that gives us the wrong impression, which can have consequences. John is a Jew. To him, the Lord's Day is on Shabbat (Saturday). Isaiah 58 reads:

> *If you turn away your foot from the Sabbath* [keep from defiling the Sabbath], *from doing your pleasure on My holy day, and call the Sabbath a delight, the holy day of the LORD honorable, and shall honor Him, not doing your own ways, nor finding your own pleasure, nor speaking your words, then you shall delight yourself in the LORD...* (Isaiah 58:13-14).

The phrase *"delight yourself in the LORD"* means to be soft and pliable before the Lord with a humble heart and teachable spirit. John was doing what the Lord required of him on Shabbat. He was seeking God through prayer and meditation when the Lord spoke to him. The Lord didn't whisper, but He spoke in a loud voice.

Once again, being a Jew, John was used to the voice of the Lord sounding like the sound of a trumpet or shofar. When the Lord brought the Hebrews out of Egypt, the Lord spoke to them through the sound of the trumpet (shofar). (See Exodus 19:13-19.) The people were so frightened by the whole experience that they asked Moses for the Lord not to speak to them again directly. (See Exodus 20:18-19.)

So one way the Lord continued to speak to them was through the use of trumpets and shofars. (See Numbers 10:1-10.) When John heard the voice of the Lord, he heard it as the sound of a trumpet or shofar. This was part of the history and heritage of his people in hearing the Word of the Lord. He knew what it meant, and it certainly got his attention.

The shofar became the most important trumpet or horn which the Lord used to communicate with His people. It is mentioned 69 times in the Hebrew Bible and numerous times in the New Testament. The shofar was, and still is, made from the horn of a kosher animal such as a goat, antelope, or gazelle. The ram's horn is primarily used because it was a ram that the Lord provided for Abraham as a sacrifice in place of Isaac. Genesis 22 reads:

> *The Abraham lifted his eyes and looked, and there behind him was a ram caught in a thicket by its horns. So Abraham went and took the ram, and offered it up for a burnt offering instead of his son* (Genesis 22:13).

An interesting Jewish tradition says that the Lord preserved the two horns from the sacrificial ram given in place of Isaac. He sounded the one horn at Sinai and will sound the other horn when He redeems His people when Messiah comes at the end of the age. For this reason, when I am writing about the use of the trumpet and the seven trumpet judgments, I use the phrase, "trumpet-shofar" to refer to these judgments and the last trumpet-shofar sound to announce the coming of Messiah Jesus. If you want to know more about the shofar, you may order my book, *The Shofar: Ancient Sounds of the Messiah,* which is available from my online bookstore at www.rbooker.com.

THE VOICE OF THE LORD (VERSE 11)

Five times in the Book of Revelation, the Lord identifies Himself as the One who transcends time and space. (See Revelation 1:8,11,17; 21:6; 22:13.) He is the Alpha and Omega, the Beginning and the End, the First and the Last. This is a continuation of what the Lord has said about Himself in the Hebrew Scriptures. (See Isaiah 41:4; 44:6; 48:12.) It is just another way of saying that He is the same "I AM" who revealed Himself to Moses at the Exodus.

As mentioned in the previous chapter, the One True God, the God of Abraham, Isaac, and Jacob revealed Himself by His name to Moses as the One who always was, always is, and always will be (see Exod. 3:14). In Hebrew, He is the *Yud-Heh-Vav-Heh (YHVH)*, the self-existing, uncaused One who transcends time and space. He is *Ehyeh Asher Ehyeh,* the One who was, who is and who is to come.

He is the Almighty One who declares the end from the beginning, as we learn in Isaiah:

> *...For I am God, and there is no other; I am God, and there is none like Me, declaring the end from the begin-ning, and from ancient times things that are not yet done, saying, "My counsel shall stand, and I will do all My plea-sure"* (Isaiah 46:9-10).

Since God is outside of time and space, He alone knows the future, and He is showing part of it to John. His purpose in doing so is for John to write what he sees in a book and send it to the seven congregations. Of course, we benefit as well since God has preserved the book for us to study for our times.

THE VISION OF THE SON OF MAN (VERSES 12-16)

When John turned to see who was talking to him, he had his vision of the Son of Man. Jesus is frequently called the "Son of Man" in the Gospels, but most of those designations refer to Him in his human-ity, not His Messianic nature and identification. Those references really should be in a lowercase designation, such as, "son of man."

However there is clearly one instance when Jesus refers to Himself by the Messianic title, "Son Man." This is recorded in Matthew when the high priest was interrogating Jesus. Matthew writes:

> *But Jesus kept silent. And the high priest answered and said to Him, "I put You under oath by the living God: tell us if You are the Christ [Messiah], the Son of God!" Jesus said to him, "It is as you said. Nevertheless, I say to you hereafter you will see the Son of Man sitting at the right*

hand of the Power, and coming on the clouds of heaven"
(Matthew 26:63-64).

Jesus answered by referring to Daniel's prophecy of the exalted Son of Man, the Messiah establishing His Messianic Kingdom on the earth. Jewish scholars often refer to the Son of Man as the "Cloud Man," since Daniel says he is coming with the clouds of Heaven.

Daniel had his own apocalyptic vision similar to John's, and wrote:

> *I was watching in the night visions, and behold, One like the Son of Man, coming with the clouds of heaven! He came to the Ancient of Days, and they brought Him near before Him. Then to Him was given dominion and glory and a kingdom, that all peoples, nations, and languages should serve Him. His dominion is an everlasting dominion, which shall not pass away, and His Kingdom the one which shall not be destroyed* (Daniel 7:13-14).

The apocalyptic book of Enoch in the Apocrypha connects to Daniel's vision with these words:

> There I beheld the Ancient of Days whose head was white like wool, and with him another, whose countenance resembled that of a man. His countenance was full of grace, like that of one of the holy angels. Then I inquired of one of the angels, who went with me, and who showed me every secret thing, concerning this Son of Man; who He was; whence He was; and why He accompanied the Ancient of days. He answered and said to me, "This is the Son of Man, to whom righteousness belongs; with whom righteousness had dwelt; and who will reveal all the treasures of that which is concealed; for the Lord of spirits has chosen Him; and His portion

has surpassed all before the Lord of spirits in everlasting righteousness" (1 Enoch 46:1-2).

John clearly understood that Jesus was the same "Son of Man" Daniel and the apocalyptic Enoch saw in their visions. Using symbols, John describes the Son of Man. Thankfully he explains some of the symbols for us. As just noted, John sees Jesus as a Jewish Messiah. He describes Him in Jewish terms, not in Christian terms. Jesus is surrounded by Jewish symbols, not Western Greco-Roman Christian symbols. In His humanity, Jesus was, is, and always will be Jewish. He came the first time as the Jewish Prophet, is now interceding as the Jewish High Priest, and will return as the Jewish King.

John sees Jesus standing in the midst of seven golden lampstands which John says represents the seven congregations (see Rev. 1:20). Jesus is dressed like the High Priest. This imagery is taken from the description of the Tabernacle of Moses and the dress of the High Priest. (See Exodus 25-40.)

The idea John wants his readers to understand is that Jesus is with them and interceding for them. He is the greater High Priest *(Cohen HaGadol)* than Aaron who ever lives to make intercession for them. Plus, He has put His Spirit *(Ruach HaKodesh)* in them as a down payment guarantee that He is not only with them but in them and that they will live forever with Him.

John not only sees Jesus as the great High Priest, He also sees Him as the Judge of Rome and the nations. His white hair, white as the snow, pictures Jesus in the same light as Daniel does the "Ancient of Days." It symbolizes His wisdom and purity that transcends time and space.

Daniel reads:

> *I watched till thrones were put in place, and the Ancient of Days was seated; His garment was white as snow, and the hair of His head was like pure wool. His throne was like a fiery flame, its wheels a burning fire; a fiery stream issued*

and came forth from before Him. A thousand thousands ministered to Him; ten thousand times ten thousand stood before Him. The court was seated, and the books were opened (Daniel 7:9-10).

With eyes like a flame of fire, the Son of Man sees all that is evil, including the emperor cult worship in Rome, and the evil of the nations of our time. He also sees the sins of the seven congregations as well as ours today.

Like modern machines that can see through our clothes and bodies and expose our hidden items and inner organs, the Lord not only sees our outward actions and words, but with His heavenly X-ray vision, He sees into our hearts. He is able to expose our motives and any hidden things. In time, He will burn up all that is unholy and purify all that is holy. His blazing eyes of fire symbolize His righteousness, which must separate, purify, and cleanse His creation and His people from all that is impure.

In the Bible, brass is a symbol of judgment. The altar where sacrifices were made at the Tabernacle was made of brass (see Exod. 27:1-8). John sees the Son of Man with feet of fine brass that have been refined in a furnace. This is John's way of saying that Jesus is able to administer a pure, righteous judgment.

In His first coming, the Son of Man came to save mankind from its sins. He came as the Lamb of God. But in His second coming, He will return as the Lion of the Tribe of Judah to judge the nations and the people of the earth. He is our Savior-Redeemer and our Judge and King. He is both the Lamb and the Lion who will judge the nations and rule over them with a rod of iron (see Ps. 2).

In spite of their suffering at the hands of the Romans and the suffering of many in our world today, God's pure and holy people will overcome our enemies and rule with the glorious Son of Man in a Kingdom characterized by righteousness and peace. God will judge the wicked and redeem those who are His.

When John hears the voice of the Son of Man, he describes it as sounding like the voice of many waters. One of the most exciting natural sights and sounds is that of a beautiful waterfall. If you are hiking toward a waterfall, all you have to do is to listen for the roar of the falls and follow the sound.

If you have ever been to Niagara Falls, you can understand what John means. The roar of Niagara Falls is so loud, you can hear it for a great distance. It is a deafening roar that literally drowns out any other noise as the water pours over the falls.

Likewise, when the voice of the Son of Man speaks, it is the roar of the Lion of Judah. His voice is so awesome and majestic that the whole world will hear His Words roar with the voice of God. He will declare judgment on the nations, but guidance, encouragement, comfort, and hope for God's people. His voice alone will be heard.

John sees Jesus holding seven stars in His right hand, which John says are the angels or messengers of the seven congregations. The Greek word translated as *angels* is also used to reference human messengers in five New Testament passages (see Matt. 11:10; Mark 1:2; Luke 7:24,27; 9:52). Most likely, John means the spiritual leaders of the seven congregations.

The fact that the Lord has them in His right hand indicates that He is protecting them and empowering them with the grace, faith, and strength they need to endure their time of testing and persecution. He will never leave them nor forsake them, but will enable them to face their challenges with His authority and refining fire working in them and through them to be a witness to the ungodly.

For modern believers, Paul's words to Timothy are for us as well:

...*"The Lord knows those who are His," and, "Let everyone who names the name of Christ* [Messiah] *depart from
iniquity"* (2 Timothy 2:19).

Using apocalyptic symbols, John says that when the Son of Man
speaks, His Words are like a sharp two-edged sword coming out of His
mouth. John is referring to the sword used by the Romans which they
developed for close hand-to-hand combat.

Previous swords used in combat were long, heavy, difficult to han-
dle, and sharp on only one side. They were wielded in a backing and
hacking motion. The Roman sword was shorter, about two feet long,
and was stronger and lighter, which allowed the Roman soldier to
attack the enemy with a slicing motion from either side of the sword.
The Roman sword was a revolutionary advance in warfare. It gave the
Roman soldier a great advantage, as it was by far a superior weapon to
that used by the enemy.

Spiritually speaking, when the Son of Man speaks, His words are
even more powerful than a Roman sword. Whereas the Roman sword
can only deal a blow to the body, the Word of God can deal a blow to
the soul.

With one side, God's words can judge, and with the other side, His
words can heal. Hebrews explains:

> For the Word of God is living and powerful, and sharper
> than any two-edged sword, piercing even to the division
> of soul and spirit, and of joints and marrow, and is a dis-
> cerner of the thoughts and intents of the heart (Hebrews
> 4:12).

Revelation 19:15 explains that when the Lord returns He will smite
the nations by the power of His spoken words: *"Now out of His mouth
goes a sharp sword, that with it He should strike the nations."*

Unlike the countenance of Jesus on the cross, John says the blazing glory and dazzling splendor of the Son of Man was like the brightness of the sun in all its brilliance. We know we cannot look at the sun directly with our natural eyes as it is too bright for us to gaze at. Likewise, the glory of the Son of Man was so bright, John could not look upon Him directly. He was so overwhelmed at the glorious countenance of the exalted Son of Man that He fell at the Lord's feet in a spiritual daze as if he were dead.

Matthew records a similar experience when Jesus gave Peter, James, and John a glimpse of His glory on the Mount of Transfiguration. Matthew says that Jesus was transfigured before them and His face shone like the sun and His clothes were as white as the light. When they saw Jesus in His blazing glory and heard God's voice, they too fell on their faces and were afraid. (See Matthew 17:1-7.) Jesus touched them and told them not to be afraid.

Lord of Life and Death (verses 17-20)

This is the second time in John's life that he has seen Jesus glorified. And the second time Jesus has touched John with that same powerful, assuring right hand and told him not to be afraid. Jesus reassures John that no matter what he and his fellow believers are going through, He (Jesus) has transcended time and space (the First and the Last), and has conquered death and the abode of the dead.

Jesus comforts John by reminding him that He is the Resurrected One who once was dead but now lives. The difference between Christianity and the other religions of the world is not necessarily the moral teachings of Christianity, because most religions have a moral code for their followers. The difference is "the empty tomb."

The founders of the other great religions of the world all died and stayed dead. Not so with Jesus. When His followers went to His tomb, they were greeted by an angel who said:

Do not be afraid, for I know that you seek Jesus who was crucified. He is not here; for He is risen, as He said. Come, see the place where the Lord lay (Matthew 28:5-6).

Yes, there is an empty tomb in Jerusalem. Because Jesus never sinned, death and *Hades* could not hold Him. He was resurrected from the dead and appeared to many of His disciples, including John.

All the emperors of Rome are dead. All the leaders of the great empires of the past are dead. All the leaders of the present world system will one day die. All the religious leaders, prophets and kings past, present and future, have died or will die. And they will stay dead until the resurrection and judgment. But not Jesus of Nazareth. He lives forever to make intercession for His people, and He will return to judge the wicked and redeem His Covenant people. Let the people of God say, "Amen!"

Jesus boldly proclaims that He has the keys of *Hades* and Death. *Hades* is the Greek word for the place of the souls of people who have died. It is the abode of the dead. The Hebrew Bible uses the word *Sheol* to identify the place of the dead. Keys are a symbol of authority. In speaking the way He did to John, Jesus is comforting John and the seven congregations that He, not the Roman emperor, has authority over life and death. Therefore, "Don't be afraid."

This is also a word of comfort for believers today. No matter what challenges we may face, Jesus has faced them all and defeated them. He faced the Roman government in Israel and defeated it. He faced persecution from religious leaders and defeated them. He faced satan and defeated him. He faced *Hades* and death and defeated it. And He promises us that same victory. We do not have to fear those who hate us and persecute us. We do not have to fear death and the grave because Jesus conquered it all for us. May His name be praised forever!

Jesus spoke of these things when He walked the Earth. He said:

Most assuredly, I say to you, he who hears My word and believes in Him who sent Me has everlasting life, and shall not come into judgment, but has passed from death into life.

Most assuredly, I say to you, the hour is coming, and now is, when the dead will hear the voice of the Son of God; and those who hear will live. For as the Father has life in Himself, so He has granted the Son to have life in Himself, and has given Him authority to execute judgment also, because He is the Son of Man.

Do not marvel at this; for the hour is coming in which all who are in the graves will hear His voice and come forth—those who have done good [what is acceptable to God] *to the resurrection of life, and those who have done evil* [what is not acceptable to God] *to the resurrection of condemnation* (John 5:24-29).

The voice of the Son of Man and Son of God is so loud and powerful that it will even awaken the dead. Those who have fought against the One True God will awaken to judgment, while God's covenant people will awaken to glory.

Daniel foresaw the resurrection of the dead at the end of the age. He wrote:

And many of those who sleep in the dust of the earth shall awake, some to everlasting life, some to shame and everlasting contempt. Those who are wise shall shine like the brightness of the firmament, and those who turn many to righteousness like the stars forever and ever (Daniel 12:2-3).

Paul encourages us with these words:

> *But thanks be to God, who gives us the victory through our Lord Jesus Christ* [Yeshua the Messiah]. *Therefore, my beloved brethren, be steadfast, immovable, always abounding in the work of the Lord, knowing that your labor is not in vain in the Lord* (1 Corinthians 15:57-58).

Now that Jesus has John's attention, He tells him to write these things he sees in his vision, including the revelation of the Son of Man, the letter to the seven congregations, and the things he will see in his later visions as described in Revelation 4:2; 17:3; and 21:10. Wow, this is so exciting. Let's join John as he shares this incredible vision that is not only for his first-century readers, but for us today.

REVIEW QUESTIONS

1. Write a summary of what you have learned in this lesson. Write the summary in clear concise words as if you are going to present it to another person.

2. Write an explanation of how you can apply what you have learned in this lesson to your life.

3. Share what you have learned with your family, friends, and members of your study group.

ENDNOTE

1. John Fox, *Fox's Book of Martyrs, or a History of the Lives, Sufferings, and Triumphant Deaths of the Primitive Protestant Martyrs,* ed. William Byron Forbush, http://www.biblestudytools.com/history/foxs-book-of-martyrs/.

Chapter 6

The Letter to Ephesus

JOHN began his writing in an apocalyptic style describing a heavenly vision. As mentioned in earlier chapters, this was a common way of writing in his time.

In his spiritual state, John had a supernatural, mystical revelation. He received a word from the Lord and saw things that explained earthly realities from a heavenly perspective. He then communicated his visions in symbolic language that the people of his day would understand.

The common theme in apocalyptic writings was that God knew of the sufferings of His people and would, in His own time, judge evil and reward the righteous. God's people should find faith to overcome their trials, and remain faithful and endure to the end. In God's time, He would reveal to them the heavenly perspective of their suffering and reward them accordingly.

In the Book of Revelation, this is communicated by Jesus giving John prophetic messages for the seven congregations in Asia Minor. Since the number seven in the Bible often symbolizes completion, we are to understand that the seven congregations were representative of typical challenges of other congregations in the general area. Many scholars believe they also are representative of congregations throughout history until the end of the age when the Messiah returns to judge the nations and honor His faithful servants.

As we study the Lord's letter to the seven congregations, we will certainly see challenges that are common to all of us no matter when or where we live. We will recognize many of the same issues in our modern congregations as well as in our personal lives. These letters are just as relevant for us today

As stated previously, the Lord may have chosen the seven particular congregations because they were leading congregations in the area and were located on the main Roman road. John gave his written revelation to a courier who left Patmos and arrived first at Ephesus. (See the map below.)

John's prophetic message was a circular document that would be read publicly to all seven of the congregations. Scholars believe that less than 20 percent of the public was literate. As a result, John's entire revelation would be read aloud to each congregation. This is one of the reasons why a special blessing was promised to those who read and hear the prophecy.

The courier would travel up the coast to Smyrna and give the prophecy to the leader of the congregation who read the entire prophecy to that congregation. The courier then continued north to Pergamos. At Pergamos, he then turned southeast to Thyatira and continued south to Sardis, Philadelphia, and finally to Laodicea.

This is the exact order in which the Lord gave the messages to John. Since the whole prophecy was read to each of the seven congregations, they all got to hear, for better or for worse, what the Lord said to each of them. Now how would we feel if others read what the Lord said to us personally?

As we read the prophetic messages to the seven congregations, we quickly see that they all follow the same well-defined structure. The Lord begins each message with a greeting which relates back to John's vision of Jesus, the Son of Man, in the heavenly scene in the first chapter. In other words, Jesus greets each congregation with an aspect of His person or His title that relates who He is to their particular circumstance. For example, Jesus reminds those in Smyrna, who were being persecuted and martyred, that He was the First and the Last and had conquered death.

Jesus then commends the congregation for the good things He can say to them. Regrettably, Jesus did not have anything good to say to the congregations at Sardis and Laodicea. These were the dead and lukewarm congregations. Jesus then gave a warning or rebuke to each congregation for their shortcomings. The Lord did not find any shortcomings with which to rebuke the congregations at Smyrna and Philadelphia. These were the persecuted and faithful congregations. Jesus then exhorted the congregations to take the appropriate action with a promise of blessings for obedience. We certainly should learn a lesson here.

What the believers were to overcome must be understood within the context of the struggles and temptations each congregation faced. Furthermore, in each letter the Lord connects the spiritual condition of the congregation with the character and reputation of the city. (For a quick glance of the Lord's letters to the seven congregations, please refer to the chart at the end of this chapter.)

With this introduction, let's get some background information about Ephesus that will help us understand why the Lord said what He did to the believers in this strategic city. Then we will study this prophetic message with a view of its practical application to our world and lives today.

BACKGROUND

The names of each city are important because they convey a spiritual message to the congregation in the city. The name *Ephesus* means "desirable." As we will learn, there was much good and desirable about the congregation in Ephesus.

When Rome established Asia Minor as a province in 129 B.C., Ephesus was chosen to be Rome's administrative center for the province. This meant that Roman government officials resided in Ephesus, presided over official Roman functions, and kept a close eye on activities in the city.

The most important city in Asia Minor, Ephesus was strategically located, having a large port on the Aegean Sea and major land-trade routes connecting the city to inland markets. As a result of its strategic location, and with a population of over 250,000, its influence rivaled Alexandria in Egypt and Antioch in Syria. Ephesus was a beautiful and prosperous city, the "San Francisco by the bay" of Asia Minor. It was easy to fall in love with Ephesus.

But there were ecological problems that, over time, had a major impact on the city. Inland deforestation in the mountain regions left much of the soil exposed. Heavy rains washed the eroded soil down to the harbor and the silt was gradually filling the harbor. Roman engineers did their best to dredge the harbor, but to no avail. By the end of the first century, the harbor had silted up. As a result, Ephesus went into decline. By the time John wrote his prophetic messages, people were losing their first love for Ephesus.

Today, the ruins of Ephesus are about seven miles from the sea. Because of its extensive ruins, Ephesus is a major tourist destination with major sites including the Basilica of St. John, the supposed house of the Virgin Mary, the Ephesus Museum, and the Great Theater.

Ephesus prided itself on being a major cultural and entertainment center, with a large stadium, a bustling marketplace, and a theater carved out of a hill that seated 25,000 people. This is where the silversmiths rioted because Paul was hurting their business of making statues of Diana. Seeing that the rioting was getting out of control, a city official calmed the people and dismissed the crowd because of fear that the local Roman proconsul might use Roman soldiers to bring order (see Acts 19:21-41).

Located outside the town, the temple to Diana was one of the Seven Wonders of the ancient world. According to historical records, the temple was 425 feet long, 220 feet wide, and had 127 columns that were 60 feet high. Since Diana was the goddess of fertility, the temple employed thousands of temple prostitutes. Merchants from the sea and pilgrims throughout the region went to Ephesus to worship at the temple. We don't need much imagination to know what this worship involved.

The citizens of Ephesus were fanatically devoted to Diana. There were Diana festivals with huge crowds participating in the idolatry and immorality associated with Diana worship. To the pagan mind, sex with temple prostitutes was a sacred act by which they expressed their desire for union with the gods and goddesses they worshiped. The festivals were one big carnival atmosphere of immorality and debauchery. Obviously, the temple and its accompanying activities was a major source of income for the city.

But more important than the temple to Diana was the temple of Domitian. As mentioned in previous chapters, it was the construction of the temple of Domitian that created a crisis for the believers in Ephesus. To review, the temple had a statue of Domitian and an altar for making sacrifices to the emperor. Citizens of Ephesus were required to bow in worship to the image of Domitian as lord god. Those who refused to do so were considered enemies of Rome and either exiled or killed.

Imperial cult worship was the way Rome united its empire. Therefore, emperor worship was the test of loyalty to the empire. Acknowledging the emperor as a god, bowing to his image, and making a sacrifice was more of a political statement than a religious one. It showed your loyalty to the empire and all that it represented, including its government, its policies, decrees, rulings, its institutions, and its culture and values. Having a Roman proconsul in Ephesus put even more pressure on the believers to bow before the emperor. It was a clear choice of allegiance to the anti-God empire of the beast (the emperor) or to the Kingdom of God.

Jews and followers of Jesus worshiped the One True God and Him only. They could not in good conscience bow to the emperor. While most resisted at the cost of being exiled or martyred, some were weak and bowed to the emperor. As you can imagine, this caused great problems between those who resisted and those who submitted. Obviously, this was a major crisis for the believers. The Lord sent His prophetic message to encourage them.

PAUL AT EPHESUS

We learn about Paul's ministry in Ephesus in Acts 19. He had been to Ephesus earlier with Priscilla and Aquila. Since he was anxious to get to Jerusalem for *Shavuot* (Pentecost), he stayed only a short time teaching at the synagogue, but left Priscilla and Aquila there to share the Gospel of the Kingdom of God (see Acts 18:18-21; 20:16).

Later, Apollos came to Ephesus to preach the Gospel. He was a powerful teacher, but he only knew about the baptism of John. When Priscilla and Aquila realized that Apollos did not have up-to-date information about the Messiah, they took him aside privately and explained to him the good news that the Messiah had come in the person of Jesus of Nazareth (see Acts 18:24-28).

Paul returned to Ephesus around A.D. 55. He found 12 disciples who only knew of John's baptism. When Paul shared the Gospel with them, they believed. Paul then baptized them as full believers. When he laid hands on them, the Holy Spirit came upon them, and they spoke in tongues and prophesied (see Acts 19:1-7).

This time, Paul stayed in Ephesus and preached the Kingdom of God for three months at the synagogue. Unfortunately, some in the synagogue resisted Paul's message, so he took the believers and rented the facility of Tyrannus where he taught daily for two years. Since Tyrannus taught in the morning, the building was vacant for Paul to teach in the afternoon. Altogether, Paul stayed in Ephesus for three years (see Acts 20:31). Because Ephesus was the gateway city to Asia Minor with many visitors, Paul's message reached the entire region (see Acts 19:8-10), and the congregation in Ephesus became the "Mother Church" for all of Asia.

God worked great miracles through Paul, so much so that Jewish exorcists who were not followers of Jesus used His name to cast out demons. When the seven sons of Sceva, a Jewish high priest, tried this, it didn't work. The demon in the man said, *"Jesus I know, and Paul I know; but who are you?"* The demon overpowered them, tore off their clothes and wounded them. They barely got away with their lives (see Acts 19:11-16).

Everyone in Ephesus heard about this, so the name of Jesus was exalted. Many of the new believers began confessing their sins, and many who practiced magic repented and burned their magic books, the value of which was 50,000 pieces of silver (see Acts 19:17-20).

So many people in Ephesus were turning to the Lord that it was hurting the business of the silversmiths who made statues of Diana to sell to the public. They gathered a large crowd at the theater and pro- voked them to riot. But a city official persuaded them to disband for fear of the Roman authorities.

After ministering in Greece, Paul returned to Ephesus and addressed the elders of the congregation. He gave a passionate address to them and exhorted them to protect the believers, because false teachers would come from without and within to pull the people away to themselves. Paul's farewell message to them and their response was one of genuine love (see Acts 20:17-38). He later wrote a letter to them while a prisoner in Rome. Paul sent Timothy to Ephesus to pastor the congregation of believers (see 1 Tim. 1:3) and wrote him two letters (see 1 and 2 Tim.). Christian tradition is that John also lived and ministered at Ephesus.

With this background, let's now see what the Lord had to say to the believers in Ephesus (see Rev. 2:1-7). John is writing around A.D. 96, which is about 40 years after Paul's ministry. There is a new generation of believers who were not around when Paul, Priscilla and Aquila, and Apollos were doing the hard pioneering work of bringing God's Word to Ephesus. The later generation, it seems, is taking for granted what the pioneers had to fight to establish.

This second generation of believers considered God's work in their midst their right rather than a privilege earned by those who went before them. This is human nature, which is why we need to be reminded of the price paid by those who have gone before us so that we can reap the benefit of what they sowed. In many instances, our spiritual forefathers and pioneers gave their lives for the blessings we enjoy. For various rea- sons, we don't think about these things, but it is so important that we remember and honor those who lived for and sacrificed for the next generations of believers. We owe our spiritual forefathers, including the faithful believers at Ephesus, so much. Let's now read the Lord's letter to these believers.

To the Congregation at Ephesus
(Revelation 2:1-7)

The Greeting (verse 1)

As stated previously, the word translated as *angel* can also mean humans. In this case, Jesus is addressing His prophetic message to the leader(s) or elders of the congregation at Ephesus.

John has explained that the seven stars symbolize the seven leaders of the seven congregations and the seven lampstands represent the seven congregations (see Rev. 1:20). The Lord refers to Himself differently in each greeting based on the problems of the congregation to whom He is writing. He says two things to them in His greeting.

First, Jesus reminds them that He holds them in His right hand. In biblical times, the right hand was considered the place of power and protection based on a covenant relationship. For example, God says to His people through Isaiah:

> *Fear not, for I am with you; be not dismayed, for I am your God. I will strengthen you, yes, I will help you, I will uphold you with My righteous right hand* (Isaiah 41:10).

Second, Jesus reminds them that He walks in the midst of them. Even though He is in Heaven and they are on the earth, He has sent them the Holy Spirit who lives in them. The Holy Spirit manifests the life and power of Jesus living in them. In the Hebrew Scriptures, God said to His people:

Have I not commanded you? Be strong and of good cour-
age; do not be afraid, nor be dismayed, for the Lord *your*
God is with you wherever you go (Joshua 1:9).

Jesus gave the following wonderful promise to His disciples:

And I will pray the Father, and He will send you another
Helper [Comforter], *that He may abide with you for-*
ever—the Spirit of truth, whom the world cannot receive,
because it neither sees Him nor knows Him; but you know
Him, for He dwells with you and will be in you (John
14:16-17).

These are certainly reassuring words of encouragement and comfort. No matter what the challenges and difficulties facing the believers
in Ephesus (and us today), we have a covenant relationship with God
who is responsible to strengthen us and empower us to overcome and
endure whatever evil comes against us. God has not forsaken His covenant people. He is with us and in us. As He said, "He will never leave
us nor forsake us" (see Heb. 13:5).

Jesus said, *"In the world you will have tribulation; but be of good*
cheer, I have overcome the world" (John 16:33). Both the Bible and history are clear that the world hates God's people. Persecution and suffering are part of the Jewish and Christian experience. The good news is
that the glorious Son of Man overcame Rome, overcame sin, overcame
satan, and overcame death. He lives in the hearts of His people and
greater is He who is in us than he who is in the world (see 1 John 4:4).

Jesus told His disciples:

Blessed are you when men revile you and persecute you,
and say all kinds of evil against you falsely for My sake.
Rejoice and be exceedingly glad, for great is your reward
in heaven, for so they persecuted the prophets who were
before you (Matthew 5:11-12).

The Commendation (verses 2-3)

The Lord has some good things to say to the congregation at Ephesus. He commends them for five aspects of their congregational life.

1. They were zealous for good works.

2. They were persevering—patiently enduring.

3. They resisted sin—did not tolerate evildoers.

4. They tested and exposed false apostles.

5. They hated the deeds of the Nicolaitans.

The congregation at Ephesus is about 40 years old. They are still "doing the work of ministry" in that they were zealous for good works. Jesus said that the works He did were proof that the Father had sent Him (see John 5:36). He told His disciples, *"Let your light so shine before men, that they may see your good works and glorify your Father in heaven"* (Matt. 5:16).

New Testament faith was a way of life. When Constantine embraced Christianity as the official religion of Rome, he changed the very essence of the faith from a lifestyle of deeds to a religion of creeds. From that time until now, Christianity, as a religion, has been based on what one believes rather than how one lives. While it is important to know why and what we believe as Christians, there is a huge difference between the Apostle's Creed (what we believe) and the Sermon on the Mount (how we live).

Many professing Christians erroneously think they are true believers just because they "believe" in Jesus. Yet, they show little if any evidence of genuine faith. For much of the Christian world, faith is a noun—it is something we believe. But to the Lord, faith is an action word—it is the way we live. In our "easy-believism" world of modern Christianity, we really need to ponder the words of James:

> *But be doers of the word, and not hearers only, deceiving*
> *yourselves... What does it profit, my brethren, if someone*
> *says he has faith but does not have works? Can faith save*
> *him?* (James 1:22; 2:14)

The Lord also commends the congregation at Ephesus for persevering through patient endurance of the crisis they faced regarding emperor worship. It would have been easy for the believers to "fix their sandals" in front of the statue of the emperor. They didn't really have to worship the emperor. It was just an outward show to appease the local Roman officials. They could have compromised and gone on with their lives. But they refused to bow to the emperor and the evil empire he represented. As a result, they were enemies of the state.

I pointed out in an earlier chapter how America was born out of a Judeo-Christian heritage. That heritage is what has made America great. Now that America despises what has made it great, we are destroying ourselves from within. Jews and Bible-believing Christians will become enemies of the state.

Like the believers at Ephesus, we too will have a choice either to accept the anti-God policies and values of the government or follow the teaching of the Bible. The Bible says that God will deliver [protect and seal] His own from His coming wrath and judgment on the earth (see 1 Thess. 1:10). His wrath and judgment are not against His own people. Regarding these times, Jesus told His disciples, *"But he who endures to the end shall be saved"* (Matt. 24:13; see also Matt. 10:22).

As America continues to turn away from God, may we live in such a way that the Lord will be able to commend us for our patient endurance in the midst of trials and tribulation. James also wrote:

> *Therefore be patient, brethren, until the coming of the*
> *Lord. See how the farmer waits for the precious fruit of*
> *the earth, waiting patiently for it until it receives the early*

and latter rain. You also be patient. Establish your hearts,
for the coming of the Lord is at hand (James 5:7-8).

The Lord also commended the congregation because they did not tolerate sin or evildoers among its members. This is a remarkable word of praise considering the fact that they lived in the city that was the center of Diana worship and all the idolatry and immorality that accompanied it. Also, as we have learned, Ephesus was a huge center for the occult. The English language uses the word *magic.* Ephesus offered many temptations and fleshly pleasures to its citizens. Yet the Lord commended the congregation for staying pure and holy.

Like Ephesus, the anti-God American culture of our day constantly bombards us with temptations that appeal to the lust of the flesh, the lust of the eyes, and the pride of life. Immorality, greed, pride, and arrogance against God is the accepted and expected way of life for many in leadership in government, business, the entertainment industry, the media, and sadly, for many in the Christian world. What at one time was considered evil is now called good, and what was good is now called evil.

As our world becomes more and more secular with no fear of God, may we live pure and holy lives that please the Lord. Perhaps John's admonition in his first letter would be a good reminder for us today:

> *Do not love the world or the things in the world. If anyone*
> *loves the world, the love of the Father is not in him. For*
> *all that is in the world—the lust of the flesh, the lust of the*
> *eyes, and the pride of life—is not of the Father but is of*
> *the world. And the world is passing away, and the lust of*
> *it; but he who does the will of God abides forever* (1 John
> 2:15-17).

The Lord further commended the congregation at Ephesus for testing and exposing false apostles. We recall that Paul warned them about this in his farewell address (see Acts 20:28-30). In Paul's first letter to Timothy, he exhorted Timothy to teach sound doctrine so the people would be firmly established in the faith and not easily led astray by false teachers.

There are also many false teachers in our Christian world today. We see them not only in the pulpit but on television and on the Internet. Jesus warned us against them with these words:

> *Beware of false prophets, who come to you in sheep's clothing, but inwardly they are ravenous wolves. You will know them by their fruits. Do men gather grapes from thornbushes or figs from thistles? Even so, every good tree bears good fruit, but a bad tree bears bad fruit. A good tree cannot bear bad fruit, nor can a bad tree bear good fruit. Every tree that does not bear good fruit is cut down and thrown into the fire. Therefore, by their fruits you will know them* (Matthew 7:15-20).

With so many false teachers who pretend to be ministers of the Lord, the words of Jesus are just as important to our world today. Human beings have a natural tendency to embrace the sensational. We are easily deceived by charisma and performance that appeals to our soul. We often fail to *"Test all things; hold fast what is good"* (1 Thess. 5:21).

According to Jesus, we should all be "fruit inspectors." We should be looking for the fruit of the Spirit in the life of the minister. We should follow those who have proven character rather than charisma. Charisma can be counterfeited; character cannot.

It is a lot more exciting to hear a good story than it is to learn doctrine. Self-help sermons appeal to the masses. Signs and wonders always draw a big crowd. Unfortunately, because our Christianity today is so shallow, Christians cannot endure sound doctrine (see 2 Tim. 4:1-4). As a result they are easily led astray.

Along with the supernatural work of the Lord, Christians must be taught sound theology. We must be firmly grounded in the foundations of our faith. Christian doctrine, when taught under the control of the Holy Spirit, can be exciting, motivating, stimulating and life-changing. Lord, convict us if we chase after signs and wonders and look to men rather than seeking You.

As a last commendation, the Lord praised the congregation for hating with righteous anger the deeds of the Nicolaitans. Who were the Nicolaitans? They were a group of professing believers who taught that the grace of God was so great, they did not have to be concerned about sin and holy living. Most likely, they participated in the sins of the townsfolk, including the idolatry and immorality associated with emperor worship and the festivals of Diana. To their credit, the believing community shunned them.

I have personally heard preachers teach this same error regarding the grace of God. Many professing believers live their lives in sin without any fear of the Lord. They know that God loves them and they accept His grace as a cover for their lawless lifestyle.

While God's grace certainly provides forgiveness for our sins, it is not a license to sin. Paul explains, *"What shall we say then? Shall we continue in sin that grace may abound? Certainly not! How shall we who died to sin live any longer in it?* (Rom. 6:1-2). In writing to the Thessalonians, Paul said, *"Abstain from every form of evil"* (1 Thess. 5:22).

God's grace is not a license to sin; it is a license to serve Him and our fellow human beings. God's grace frees us from ourselves. God's grace liberates us from sin, not *to sin*. Paul explains to the Galatian believers:

> *Stand fast therefore in the liberty by which Christ [Messiah] has made us free, and do not be entangled again with a yoke of bondage...For you, brethren, have been called to liberty; only do not use liberty as an opportunity for*

the flesh, but through love serve one another (Galatians 5:1,13).

May all of God's people abstain from every form of evil. May we live our lives to please our Lord in every word, thought, and deed. May we make God glad and not sad by the way we live our lives.

The Rebuke (verses 4-6)

While the Lord had many good things to say to the believing community at Ephesus, He did have one rebuke. He said they had "left their first love." What did He mean by this?

As I have mentioned, by the time the Lord sent this prophetic message to the believers at Ephesus, the congregation had been in existence for about 40 years. They have been faithful in maintaining sound doctrine, but their zeal and passion for the Lord Himself had begun to wane. They had sound teaching and pure doctrine, but their hearts had grown cold. This was the same thing that was happening to the visitors and citizens of Ephesus as the harbor was filled with silt. It was no longer "love at first sight."

The Lord warns them that if they do not repent and rekindle their passion for Him, He will remove their lampstand. This is most likely a reference to when Titus conquered Jerusalem in A.D. 70 and removed the lampstand from the Temple and took it to Rome. The people would have understood this as there was a victory arch (the Arch of Titus) in Rome showing the Romans taking away the lampstand.

This congregation may continue their existence and carry on with their religious activities, but God's Spirit will no longer be in their midst. Their light will go out. They will "have church" and not even know that the Lord is not there.

Now, anyone who has been in love for a long time can understand what the Lord is saying to this congregation. When human beings first fall in love, all they can think about and talk about is their new love. Driven by their zeal and passion (hormones?), they want to spend every moment with the one with whom they have fallen in love. If their relationship works out, they marry and learn to live together as husband and wife.

Over time, their love relationship deepens and matures. Oftentimes, however, the romantic passion and zeal they have for one another is diminished by the familiarity of living together. As some might say, "the honeymoon is over." This is why married couples sometimes attend seminars and retreats or renew their vows in an effort to "rekindle their first love." Or they leave the children at home and go on a "romantic getaway." If they don't keep their relationship fresh and exciting, they may have a cold, loveless marriage. In other words, their "lampstand," or fire, as we call it, may go out.

Spiritually speaking, this is what has happened to the congregation at Ephesus. They love the Lord but they have lost their passion and zeal for Him. Their focus is on their theology and right doctrine rather than on the Lord Himself. We might say their spiritual hormones have grown cold. Their spiritual fire has gone out. Jesus is calling them to repent and renew their passion for Him.

This is clearly a prophetic word for us today. It is easy for Christian denominations and local congregations (and individual believers) to love their theology more than they love the Lord and other people. Oftentimes, their basis for fellowship is that we agree with their doctrines and statements of faith rather than our common love for Jesus.

While sound teaching and pure doctrine are certainly important, it must be balanced with genuine love and passion for the Lord and for other people. Otherwise, it becomes cold, judgmental, and uncaring. God's Spirit will no longer be present when they meet. They have religion without a relationship. There are many local congregations that "have church" and don't know God is no longer there.

The core teaching of the Bible from Genesis to Revelation is love for God and love for people. The great declaration of faith in the Hebrew Bible is:

Hear, O Israel: the LORD our God, the LORD is one. You shall love the LORD your God will all your heart, with all your soul, and with all your strength (Deuteronomy 6:4-5).

Since true love for God will be evidenced by our love for other people, God adds that we are to love our neighbor and the stranger as ourselves (see Lev. 19:18,34).

When a religious leader asked Jesus what He considered the greatest of God's commandments, Jesus referred to these statements about loving God and loving people (see Mark 12:30; Luke 10:27). In the Mark reference, the religious leader noted that loving God and loving people were more important than religious activities done out of duty.

Jesus said that the witness to our relationship to Him was not our doctrine but our love:

A new commandment I give to you, that you love one another; as I have loved you, that you also love one another. By this all will know that you are My disciples, if you have love for one another (John 13:34-35).

John wrote:

Beloved, let us love one another, for love is of God; and everyone who loves is born of God and knows God. He who does not love does not know God, for God is love... And we have known and believed the love that God has for us. God is love, and he who abides in love abides in God, and God in him (1 John 4:7-8,16).

John then adds:

If someone says, "I love God," and hates his brother, he is a liar; for he who does not love his brother whom he has seen, how can he love God whom he has not seen? And this commandment we have from Him: that he who loves God loves his brother also (1 John 4:20-21).

Many people may say that they love God. Many people may say that they love you. But the proof is in their attitudes and actions. John made it very clear with these words, *"My little children, let us not love in word or in tongue, but in deed and in truth"* (1 John 3:18).

The Promise (verse 7)

The Lord ends each of His prophetic messages with an exhortation to the listeners to hear His Words and a promise to those who overcome (do what the Lord says). For the believers at Ephesus, the Lord's promise is that they will *"eat from the tree of life, which is in the midst of the Paradise of God"* (Rev. 2:7).

In His blessing promise, Jesus refers to the tree of life in the Garden of Eden. The word *Paradise* refers to this garden. It means the same as the Garden of Eden.

The Lord placed two literal trees in the Garden of Eden—the tree of life and the tree of the knowledge of good and evil (see Gen. 2:9). The tree of life represented eternal life and fellowship with God, while the tree of the knowledge of good and evil represented self-enthronement and independence from God. God forbade Adam and Eve to eat from the tree of the knowledge of good and evil. Unfortunately, as we know, satan tempted Adam and Eve to disobey and they ate from the tree.

Because of their disobedience, Adam and Eve were banished from the Garden of Eden and the presence of God. Otherwise, they would have continued access to the tree of life and would live forever in their sinful condition. That truly would be tragic.

Since they could no longer eat of the tree of life, they were separated from God and eventually died. The bad news is that we have all inherited their curse of sin and death, and the sickness, sorrow, and heartache that it brings. While much of the world does not believe the Genesis account, there is really no other explanation for the condition of our world and the way human beings behave.

The good news is that the Son of Man has conquered satan, sin, and death. He has overcome it all and promises to restore full fellowship and eternal life with God to all who overcome with Him. His victory is ours. We are more than conquerors. We have overcome by the blood of the Lamb and the word of our testimony (see Rev. 12:11). Hallelujah!

This final restoration to the Garden Paradise of God and the tree of life is described in the last chapter of the Book of Revelation. This is when the One True God comes down from Heaven to once again walk among His people as He did with Adam and Eve before they sinned (see Gen. 3:8).

John writes:

> *And he showed me a pure river of water of life, clear as crystal, proceeding from the throne of God and of the Lamb. In the middle of its street, and on either side of the river, was the tree of life, which bore twelve fruits, each tree yielding its fruit every month. The leaves of the tree were for the healing of the nations.*
>
> *And there shall be no more curse, but the throne of God and of the Lamb shall be in it, and His servants shall serve Him. They shall see His face, and His name shall be on their foreheads. There shall be no night there: they need no lamp nor light of the sun, for the Lord God gives them light. And they shall reign forever and ever* (Revelation 22:1-5).

If the Lord's message to Ephesus applies to your organization, your ministry, or your life, let us repent and do what He says. Let us heed the words of Jesus who said:

"You shall love the LORD your God with all your heart, with all your soul, and with all your mind " This is the first and greatest commandment. And the second is like it: "You shall love your neighbor as yourself." On these two commandments hang all the Law and the Prophets (Matthew 22:37-40).

He who has an ear, let him hear.

REVIEW QUESTIONS

1. Write a summary of what you have learned in this lesson. Write the summary in clear concise words as if you are going to present it to another person.

2. Write an explanation of how you can apply what you have learned in this lesson to your life.

3. Share what you have learned with your family, friends, and members of your study group.

LETTERS TO THE SEVEN CONGREGATIONS OF REVELATION

	EPHESUS 2:1-7 (LEGALISTIC)	SMYRNA 2:8-11 (PERSECUTED)	PERGAMOS 2:12-17 (COMPROMISING)	THYATIRA 2:18-29 (TOLERANT)	SARDIS 3:1-6 (DEAD)	PHILADELPHIA 3:7-13 (FAITHFUL)	LAODICEA 3:14-23 (LUKEWARM)
GREETING	HOLDS STARS WALKS IN MIDST	FIRST AND LAST DEAD YET LIVES	2-EDGED SWORD	EYES LIKE FIRE FEET LIKE BRASS	7 SPIRITS 7 STARS	HOLY AND TRUE KEY OF DAVID	AMEN FAITHFUL AND TRUE WITNESS BEG. OF CREATION
COMENDATION	ZEALOUS OF WORKS PATIENT ENDURANCE NOT TOLERATE SIN EXPOSE FALSE TEACHERS HATE DEEDS OF NICOLAITANS	FAITHFUL IN TRIBULATION AND POVERTY	HELD FAST HIS NAME DID NOT DENY FAITH	LOVE SERVICE FAITH PATIENCE	—	KEPT MY WORD NOT DENIED MY NAME	—
REBUKE	LEFT FIRST LOVE	—	TOLERATED DOCTRINES OF BALAAM AND NICOLAITANS	PERMITTED UNGODLY TEACHING	YOU ARE DEAD	—	LUKEWARM SPUE OUT OF MOUTH
EXHORTATION	REMEMBER REPENT DO	DO NOT FEAR BE FAITHFUL UNTO DEATH	REPENT	REPENT HOLD FAST	WATCH STRENGTHEN REMEMBER HOLD FAST REPENT	HOLD FAST	BUY PURE GOLD WHITE RAIMENT ANOINT EYES REPENT
PROMISE	EAT OF THE TREE OF LIFE	NOT HURT BY SECOND DEATH	EAT HIDDEN MANNA WHITE STONE WITH NEW NAME	POWER OVER NATIONS RULE WITH IRON ROD MORNING STAR	CLOTHED IN WHITE BOOK OF LIFE CONFESS NAME	PILLAR IN TEMPLE A NEW NAME	SIT WITH MESSIAH ON HIS THRONE

Chapter 7

The Letter to Smyrna

REVELATION REVIEW

BECAUSE the believers were being persecuted, the Lord wanted to encourage them as well as challenge them in areas where they were failing to live up to their high calling. He introduced Himself as the exalted Son of Man in a way that related to their individual situations, both physically and spiritually. He gave each congregation a word of promise to the overcomers and a warning of consequences if they did not obey His instructions.

It is most important that we realize His words of promise were not to those who failed to repent. The Lord only had harsh words to those who were carnal and lukewarm in their commitment. The Lord did not give any of these congregations a watered down, seeker-friendly, entertaining message. The very survival of the Lord's work in the city depended on the believers responding positively to what the Lord told them. He promised blessings to the overcomers but chastening to those who did not heed His message.

The Lord had some wonderful things to say to the believers at Ephesus. He greeted them as the "One who was in their midst." He encouraged them for their good works, for their patient endurance, for not tolerating sin, for testing and exposing false apostles, and for hating the deeds of the Nicolatians. This is a wonderful spiritual "pat on the back" that we would all be grateful to hear from the Lord. When believers stand before God, the one thing we hope to hear Him say is, "Well done, good and faithful servant."

Even though the Lord had many good things to say to the believers at Ephesus, He also had a warning—they had left their first love. They had many good qualities but had grown cold in their relationship to the Lord.

This is certainly a relevant message for us today. We too often substitute religious activities and programs for a personal and intimate relationship with our Lord. We can become so busy serving God that we fail to spend time with God. There are many deeds we do that are good but not necessarily from the prompting of the Holy Spirit. For many of us, we need to spend a little less time doing what seems right to us and a little more time in the presence of God. We would get a lot more rest and not grow as weary in well doing. May we heed the words of our Lord so that we will be counted among the overcomers who will eat from the tree of life which is in the Paradise of God.

As we contemplate the Lord's words to the believers at Ephesus, let's journey along with the courier to the city of Smyrna. Before reading the Lord's letter to the believers, let's first learn some background about the city.

BACKGROUND

As mentioned previously, the seven congregations were located on one of the main Roman postal routes of their time. After taking John's letter to be read at Ephesus, the courier went to Smyrna, which was about 35 miles north of Ephesus.

The name *Smyrna* is taken from the word *myrrh*. Myrrh was one of the most important spices in ancient times. It was a bittersweet gum resin that oozed from a shrub tree. While it had a bitter taste, people used it as a sweet-smelling perfumed spice or medicine. It was often used with frankincense to anoint bodies. It had preserving characteristics that slowed the corrupting process on dead bodies.

In the New Testament, myrrh was connected to Jesus on three occasions. When the wise men from the East found Joseph, Mary, and the baby Jesus, they gave them gifts of gold, frankincense and myrrh (see Matt. 2:11). When Jesus was crucified, He was given wine mixed with myrrh, but He refused to drink it (see Mark 15:23). Nicodemus brought 100 pounds of myrrh and aloes to anoint Jesus' body for burial (see John 19:39).

Like Ephesus, Smyrna was an important seaport city on the Aegean coast. It had a protected harbor and was geographically located where the Hermes River emptied into the sea. This provided a major inland waterway, connecting trade of goods from Greek merchant ships to Asian land merchants. The city was also located on a major trade route through the Hermes valley. As with other Greek cities, Smyrna had a large library, a public theater, and a stadium that seated about 20,000 people.

Because of the advantages of its location, Smyrna was a beautiful, wealthy city and major rival to Ephesus. When the harbor at Ephesus silted up, Smyrna became the "Beautiful Ornament of Asia." Geographically, it was an important location for a believing community that would influence both East and West with the message of Jesus.

In its earliest known history, Smyrna had been a prominent city, but due to conquests and conflicts, it was reduced to a small, insignificant village. However, when Alexander the Great conquered the area, he reestablished Smyrna, at which time Smyrna regained its prominence. In other words, Smyrna died but came back to life. Alexander's successors greatly enhanced and enlarged it into a beautiful Greek city.

Smyrna was designed in such a way that it had tier after tier of houses beginning on the low ground near the harbor and rising up the hillside to the top of a hill on which stood the main public buildings. The design of the city resembled a crown, with the very top being called the "Crown of Smyrna."

When Antiochus the Great of Syria (father of Antiochus Epiphanes) threatened to attack Smyrna, the city turned to Rome for protection. As a way of bonding with Rome, Smyrna became the first Asian city to build a temple to the goddess of Rome. Later they built a temple to Tiberius, which established the cult of emperor worship at Smyrna. There were also statues and altars to different Greek gods. Smyrna was a major center of cult worship. Scholars estimate that the population of Smyrna in the first century exceeded 100,000.

The modern city of Izmir is located at the ruins of ancient Smyrna. Izmir is the third largest city in Turkey with a population of approximately 2.5 million. It is also the second largest port. Izmir is a beautiful cosmopolitan city and considered the most westernized city of Turkey. Its main archeological sites are the Church of Polycarp, the Museum, and the Agora. How interesting that a remnant of the "persecuted congregation" still functions today in Izmir.

To the Congregation at Smyrna
(Revelation 2:8-11)

Greeting (verse 8)

With this background, let's now see what the Son of Man had to say to the believers at Smyrna. We are in awe to learn that the Lord had no rebuke for these believers. Keep in mind that this prophetic message would be read aloud to all seven congregations, not just the believers at Smyrna. Each congregation would know the situation in the other congregations and what the Lord had to say to them.

Addressing His letter to the leader of the congregation in Smyrna, the Lord greets them in ways that relate to the conditions of the believers in Smyrna. They are a poor, persecuted congregation enduring severe persecution and martyrdom for their faith. In view of their difficult circumstances, the Lord speaks to their needs and refers to Himself in three ways: 1) the First and Last, 2) who was dead, 3) and came to life.

As noted already, in each of His greetings to the congregations, the Lord refers to the statements He made about Himself to John as recorded in the first chapter. In this instance, because of their suffering, the Lord greets them with His earlier revelation given to John and recorded in Revelation 1:17-18.

We have learned in Exodus 3:14 that the God of Abraham, Isaac and Jacob identified Himself in this way to Moses as *YHVH*, the One who was, who is, and who is to come. He also referred to Himself as the First and the Last. (See Isaiah 41:4; 44:6; 48:12.) The First and the Last means the same as the Alpha and Omega, the Beginning and the End. Jesus also refers to Himself by these phrases. (See Revelation 1:11; 21:6; 22:13.)

These and similar phrases simply mean that God is outside of time and knows and declares the end from the beginning. (See Isaiah 46:9-10.) By appropriating these phrases to Himself, Jesus is clearly claiming to be more than just a human. He is the divine Son of God and Son of Man. He is God in human flesh. He is one with God our Father in Heaven, but also separate from Him in His divine-human nature. This should not be so hard for us to understand. A human son is one with his father because his father's life is in him, but he is also a separate human being from his father.

The God of all creation who transcends time and space is certainly able to stay in Heaven while at the same time entering the human race to perfectly reveal Himself to us and to redeem us. Jesus claims to be that perfect human who fully embodied the nature of His Father, while at the same time redeeming us from our sins. Christians do not worship three Gods. We worship the One True God of Abraham, Isaac, and Jacob, who has fully and completely revealed Himself to us through a person, Jesus of Nazareth.

As I said, we should be able to understand this through the miracle of childbirth. A son usually bears a resemblance to his father. He looks and talks and acts like his father. He has the same characteristics and mannerisms of His father. He is one with his father, but separate from his father. He has his father's DNA but he is not the same as his father.

Likewise, Jesus had a miracle birth born of the seed of His Father in Heaven. The DNA of God was and is fully in Him. He is His Father's Son, but He is not the Father. Since He is the Son of the Almighty, He has the same characteristics of His Father—He is the First and the Last, the Alpha and the Omega, the Beginning and the End.

As with some in Smyrna who were martyred for the faith, Jesus also was martyred. He died. And to prove He was dead, His Father kept Him in a tomb for three days and three nights. Why was it so important that Jesus be in the tomb for a full three days and three nights?

Jesus told His disciples that He would be dead for three days and three nights to fulfill the sign of Jonah. In Matthew, Jesus says, *"For as Jonah was three days and three nights in the belly of the great fish, so will the Son of Man be three days and three nights in the heart of the earth"* (Matt. 12:40).

Jesus said three days and three nights. Whenever the Bible connects days and nights with the word "and," it means the full 24-hour period. So three days and three nights mean a 72-hour period of time.

You see, in Bible times, people believed that when someone died, their spirit or soul hovered over their body for three days and three nights, deciding if it wanted to depart to the next world or return to the body. This means that in the New Testament a person (Jesus, for example) was not considered fully dead until the passing of 72 hours. From a cultural understanding, Jesus had to be in the tomb for a full 72 hours. This is the reason why Jesus delayed going to Bethany when He learned that Lazarus had died.

John tells the story:

> *So when He [Jesus] heard that he [Lazarus] was sick, He stayed two more days in the place where He was…So when Jesus came, He found that he [Lazarus] had already been in the tomb four days…Jesus said, "Take away the stone." Martha, the sister of him who was dead, said to Him, "Lord, by this time there is a stench, for he has been dead four days"* (John 11:6,17,39).

Without understanding the cultural background to this story, we would miss the whole point of why Jesus delayed for two days, why John informs us that Lazarus had been in the tomb four days, and why Martha would say that her brother was dead. Jesus delayed so that everyone would know that Lazarus was really and truly dead.

Jesus did this in order to prepare people for His own death, burial, and resurrection. He had to be in the tomb a full three days and three nights for everyone to understand that He was dead. He did not faint, He did not swoon, He did not lose consciousness—He died, and His body was put in a tomb. Like the myrrh of Smyrna, Jesus' death was bittersweet. His suffering and death were certainly bitter, but His resurrection was sweet.

Because Jesus had never sinned, He was not going to stay in that tomb. That is why He used a borrowed tomb—He wasn't going to need it for very long. He didn't really need 100 pounds of myrrh to slow down the corruption of His body, because His body was not going to experience corruption.

Jesus knew this because His Father had written this as a prophecy through King David. The prophecy reads:

Therefore my heart is glad, and my glory [soul] *rejoices; my flesh also will rest in hope. For You will not leave my soul in Sheol* [the abode of the dead], *nor will You allow Your Holy One to see corruption* [decay of the body due to sin] (Psalms 16:9-10).

Since Jesus had never sinned, death had no claim on Him. As the city of Smyrna came back to life, Jesus told the believers at Smyrna that "He came to life" (see Rev. 2:8). As citizens of a resurrected city, they would understand what He meant. After He had fully fulfilled the sign of Jonah, Jesus came forth from the tomb in resurrection life and power. The timing of His death, burial, and resurrection is difficult for Western people to understand, because the biblical day (the next 24-hour period) actually begins in the evening. For a detailed explanation of the timing of the death, burial, and resurrection of Jesus according to the biblical calendar, please order my book, *Celebrating Jesus in the Biblical Feasts,* which is available from my online bookstore. Matthew gives the following account of Jesus' resurrection:

Now after the Sabbath [at the end or close of the Sabbath], *as the first day of the week began to dawn* [just as it began to get dark], *Mary Magdalene and the other Mary came to see the tomb. And behold, there was a great earthquake; for an angel of the Lord descended from heaven, and came and rolled back the stone from the door, and sat on it.*

His countenance was like lightning, and his clothing as white as snow. And the guards shook for fear of him, and became like dead men. But the angel answered and said to the women, "Do not be afraid, for I know that you seek Jesus, who was crucified. He is not here; for He is risen, as He said. Come, see the place where the Lord lay" (Matthew 28:1-6).

Jesus not only rose from the dead, but He ascended to Heaven where He now sits in the place of power and glory as the exalted Son of Man. And because He lives, the believers at Smyrna who have been martyred, as well as God's people throughout history who have given their lives for the faith, will also be raised from the dead and live forever with Him.

Our life as believers is also bittersweet. We too experience the bitterness of suffering for our faith, but the joy of knowing and serving our God is sweet. No matter what challenges we may have in the future as believers, we will overcome satan, we will overcome sin, and we will overcome death. When we die, our bodies will also rest in the hope of being resurrected. As Paul writes:

> *But if the Spirit of Him who raised Jesus from the dead dwells in you, He who raised Christ [Messiah] from the dead will also give life to your mortal bodies through His Spirit who dwells in you (Romans 8:11).*

Paul writes to the believers at Corinth:

> *Behold, I tell you a mystery; we shall not all sleep, but we shall all be changed—in a moment, in the twinkling of an eye, at the last trumpet. For the trumpet will sound, and the dead will be raised incorruptible, and we shall be changed. For this corruptible must put on incorruption, and this mortal must put on immortality. So when this corruptible has put on incorruption, and this mortal has put on immortality, then shall be brought to pass the saying that is written: "Death is swallowed up in victory. O Death, where is your sting? O Hades, where is your victory?"*

The sting of death is sin, and the strength of sin is the law. But thanks be to God, who gives us the victory through our Lord Jesus Christ [Yeshua the Messiah]. *Therefore, my beloved brethren, be steadfast, immovable, always abounding in the work of the Lord, knowing that your labor is not in vain in the Lord* (1 Corinthians 15:51-58).

We also learn in Paul's letter to the believers at Thessalonica:

But I do not want you to be ignorant, brethren, concerning those who have fallen asleep, lest you sorrow as others who have no hope. For if we believe that Jesus died and rose again, even so God will bring with Him those who sleep in Jesus. For this we say to you by the word of the Lord, that we who are alive and remain until the coming of the Lord will by no means precede those who are asleep.

For the Lord Himself will descend from heaven with a shout, with the voice of an archangel, and with the trumpet of God. And the dead in Christ [Messiah] *will rise first. Then we who are alive and remain shall be caught up together with them in the clouds to meet the Lord in the air. And thus we shall always be with the Lord* (1 Thessalonians 4:13-17).

In a further word of comfort, Paul wrote:

For God did not appoint us to wrath, but to obtain salvation through our Lord Jesus Christ [Yeshua the Messiah], *who died for us, that whether we wake or sleep, we should live together with Him. Therefore, comfort each other and edify one another, just as you also are doing* (1 Thessalonians 5:9-11).

When Lazarus died, his sister came to Jesus for comfort. John recorded the following conversation:

> *Now Martha, as soon as she heard that Jesus was coming, went and met Him, but Mary was sitting in the house. Then Martha said to Jesus, "Lord, if You had been here, my brother would not have died. But even now I know that whatever you ask of God, God will give You." Jesus said to her, "Your brother will rise again." Martha said to Him, "I know that he will rise again in the resurrection at the last day." Jesus said to her, "I am the resurrection and the life. He who believes in Me, though he may die, he shall live. And whoever lives and believes in Me shall never die. Do you believe this?"* (John 11:20-26).

Job expressed this hope for believers of all ages when he said:

> *For I know that my Redeemer lives, and He shall stand at last on the earth; and after my skin is destroyed, this I know, that in my flesh I shall see God* (Job 19:25-26).

The Commendation (verse 9)

Jesus has only praise for the congregation at Smyrna. He mentions four things about their situation and encourages them by telling them that He knows these things.

1. He knows their works.

2. He knows their tribulation.

3. He knows their poverty.

4. He know those who are persecuting them.

The Lord first mentions their works. The apostle Paul clarified that we are not saved to the Lord by our works. Most believers are taught early in our faith Paul's word to the Ephesians:

> *For by grace you have been saved through faith, and that not of yourselves; it is the gift of God, not of works, lest anyone should boast* (Ephesians 2:8-9).

In this statement, Paul is talking about religious works and the good things we do in our own strength to earn God's favor. He does not mean that we should *not* live holy lives of love, kindness, compassion, mercy, forgiveness, generosity, and righteous deeds. Paul's statements on grace and faith have been so emphasized that we have missed Paul's other statements that true faith is evidenced by works of covenantal loving-kindness produced in us, through us, and out of us by the motivation and power of the Holy Spirit.

This same Paul wrote to Titus warning him about people who claimed to be believers although their lives proved otherwise. He said, *"They profess to know God, but in works deny Him, being abominable, disobedient, and disqualified for every good work"* (Titus 1:16).

He also said in his same letter to Titus that, as we look for the coming of the Lord, we should be *"...zealous for good works"* (Titus 2:14).

Finally, in case anyone reading his letter to Titus missed his point, he concluded his letter with these words:

> *This is a faithful saying, and these things I want to affirm constantly, that those who have believed in God should be careful to maintain good works. These things are good and profitable to men...And let our people also learn to maintain good works, to meet urgent needs, that they may not be unfruitful* (Titus 3:8,14).

The believers at Smyrna had good works. This should be especially true of believers living in the endtime, as it is our deeds, not our creeds, which bear witness that our faith is genuine and not just talk. May we live our lives in such a way that the Son of Man will also commend us for our Holy Spirit-inspired works of loving-kindness. Or as Paul said:

> *For we are His workmanship, created in Christ Jesus* [Messiah Yeshua] *for good works, which God prepared beforehand that we should walk in them* (Ephesians 2:10).

Jesus also comforted them by telling them that He knew of their tribulation and suffering. The believers at Smyrna were being persecuted for their faith. Like the city where they lived, their lives were bittersweet. Smyrna was spiritually connected to Rome and the Roman gods. The believers were spiritually connected to Heaven and the God of Heaven. Smyrna was connected to the emperor. The believers were connected to the Messiah. There was a clash of kingdoms—the kingdom of Rome against the Kingdom of God. The government of Rome and the government of Heaven were in a battle for the soul of Smyrna, and the believers were at the heart of the struggle. Is Caesar Lord or is Jesus Lord?

The believers said that Jesus is Lord, and many paid for that confession with their lives. The most famous martyr in Smyrna was Polycarp. Polycarp was a disciple of John and the bishop of the congregation at Smyrna in the second century. During one of the pagan festivals, the cry went out to find Polycarp and execute him. The following information including Polycarp's prayer can be found on any work about the martyrdom of Polycarp. It is readily available from many sources.

Around A.D. 155, when he was brought before the Roman proconsul, Polycarp was given the choice of confessing Caesar and denying Jesus. His response was that he had served the Lord for 86 years and the Lord had done him no wrong, so how could he now deny Him? When the crowd heard Polycarp confess his allegiance to Jesus as opposed to Caesar, meaning Rome, they demanded that the lions be let loose to eat him. But since that part of the "entertainment" was over, they demanded that Polycarp be burned alive at the stake. When it appeared that the fire could not touch Polycarp, the executioner stabbed him to death.

With his last words, Polycarp offered this prayer to God:

> O Lord God Almighty, the Father of your beloved and blessed Son Jesus Christ [Yeshua the Messiah], through whom we have received the knowledge of you, the God of angels and powers and of all creation and of the whole race of the righteous, who live in your presence; I bless you for you have granted me this day and hour, that I might receive a portion amongst the number of martyrs in the cup of Christ [Messiah] unto resurrection of eternal life, both of soul and body, in the incorruptibility of the Holy Spirit.
>
> May I be received among these in your presence this day, as a rich and acceptable sacrifice, as you did prepare and reveal it beforehand, and have accomplished it, you that are the faithful and true God. For this cause, yes, and for all things, I praise you, I bless you, I glorify you, through the eternal and Heavenly high priest, your beloved Son, through whom with him and the Holy Spirit be glory both now and for ages to come. Amen.[1]

John says that the persecuted believers *"overcame him by the blood of the Lamb and by the word of their testimony, and they did not love their lives to the death"* (Rev. 12:11). This is the testimony that millions of martyrs down through the ages have in Heaven. If required of us, may we have that same testimony.

Christians living in America who have never suffered for their faith may find it difficult to empathize with these believers in Smyrna. However, the experience of the believers in Smyrna has been the norm for Christians throughout history. America has been the one exception because of our Judeo-Christian heritage.

As the institutions of America grow to despise our biblical heritage, the judgments of God on our nation will become more profound and more frequent with devastating consequences for the nation. Jews and Bible-believing Christians will be blamed for our calamities, and persecution will follow. May the spirit of Polycarp rest upon us all.

Peter tells us how to respond:

> *But even if you should suffer for righteousness sake, you are blessed. "And do not be afraid of their threats, nor be troubled." But sanctify the Lord God in your hearts, and always be ready to give a defense to everyone who ask you a reason for the hope that is in you, with meekness and fear* [respect]... (1 Peter 3:14-15).

We don't normally think of suffering as a blessing. However, Peter explains that suffering is a blessing because it is evidence of our godly lives. And we should not be surprised, but expect it. We don't necessarily welcome suffering; it just comes with living a righteous life.

Here is how Peter says it:

> *Beloved, do not think it strange concerning the fiery trial which is to try you, as though some strange thing happened to you; but rejoice to the extent that you partake of Christ's [Messiah's] suffering, that when His glory is revealed, you may also be glad with exceeding joy. If you are reproached for the name of Christ [Messiah], blessed are you, for the Spirit of glory and of God rests upon you. On their part He is blasphemed, but on your part He is*

glorified...Therefore let those who suffer according to the will of God commit their souls to Him in doing good, as to a faithful Creator (1 Peter 4:12-14,19).

Peter went on to say that God uses suffering to test our faith and that it is only for a little while. It pales in comparison to the eternal glory God has reserved for us in Heaven. Peter explains:

Blessed be the God and Father of our Lord Jesus Christ [Yeshua the Messiah], *who according to His abundant mercy has begotten us again to a living hope through the resurrection of Jesus Christ* [Yeshua the Messiah] *from the dead, to an inheritance incorruptible and undefiled and that does not fade away, reserved in heaven for you, who are kept by the power of God through faith for salvation ready to be revealed in the last time.*

In this you greatly rejoice, though now for a little while, if need be, you have been grieved [distressed] *by various trials, that the genuineness of your faith, being much more precious than gold that perishes, though it be tested by fire, may be found to praise, honor, and glory at the revelation of Jesus Christ* [Yeshua the Messiah], *whom having not seen you love. Though now you do not see Him, yet believing, you rejoice with joy inexpressible and full of glory, receiving the end of your faith—the salvation of your souls* (1 Peter 1:3-9).

In addition to their persecution, the believers were also in great poverty. There was a "spy and reward" network in Smyrna that was very lucrative for those who reported the believers to the authorities. This is often the case where there is a totalitarian government that is threatened by dissent. The local "community organizers," or spies, were given a percentage of the property and assets of those they reported to the authorities.

Further contributing to their poverty was a boycott against buying goods and services from the believers. This would have greatly affected the ability of the believers to survive, much less prosper. We see this later in John's revelation, where only those who had the Mark of the Beast could do business (see Rev. 13:16-18).

As our nation continues to crumble economically, American believers will face similar challenges from what I believe is an anti-God government. Due to hyperinflation and the devaluation of our currency, we may see the time when we have to work all day just to get enough money to buy a loaf of bread (see Rev. 6:5-6). Yet even in the most trying of times, the Lord promises to meet our needs (see Phil. 4:19).

The Lord's words of comfort to the believers at Smyrna are just as relevant for us today. He reminds them that they are rich with spiritual blessings that cannot be taken from them. His Words in Matthew are appropriate for believers everywhere who have lost their finances due to their righteous witness:

> *Do not lay up for yourselves treasures on earth, where moth and rust destroy and where thieves break in and steal; but lay up for yourselves treasures in heaven, where neither moth nor rust destroys, and where thieves do not break in and steal. For where your treasure is, there your heart will be also* (Matthew 6:19-21).

Finally, the Son of Man says He knows those who are persecuting them. Since He knows who is persecuting them, the implication is that He will judge them in His own appointed time. Those who are being persecuted will be rewarded, while those doing the persecuting will be judged.

Jesus says that the ones causing the believers so much grief are a group of people who say they are Jews but are not really Jews. Jesus says they are a *"synagogue of satan"* (Rev. 2:9). Unfortunately, Western scholars have used this Scripture and a similar one in Revelation 3:9 to justify anti-Semitism.

The traditional interpretation is that these are nonbelieving Jews. This is the explanation in the footnotes of your Bible and is one of the reasons why some believe the New Testament to be anti-Semitic. While it may be true that these are Jews, the reality is that we don't really know who Jesus is talking about. Jesus says they claim to be Jews but are not Jews.

In the first century, as in our times, there were religious groups who claimed to be Jews but were not Jews. In our own times, the Mormons claim to be descendants of the Ten Lost Tribes of Israel and teach that everyone who is not a Mormon, including Jews, is a Gentile. The British Israelite movement considered the British to be the Ten Lost Tribes of Israel. Some consider the Native Americans to be the Ten Lost Tribes. Others teach that Christians who love Israel and their Jewish roots are Jews. There is a group from America who called themselves "Black Hebrews." They have moved to Israel and been given certain recognition by the Israeli government. Can all of these groups who are not Jews, but call themselves Jews, be Jews?

To make this more confusing, the English translation uses the word *synagogue* to identify the persecutors. When we read the word synagogue, we automatically associate it with Jews. But synagogue is a bad translation. Instead of synagogue, the word should be translated as *congregation* or *assembly* as it is in James 2:2.

Furthermore, in James 5:14 when James says the sick should call for the elders of the church for prayer, the word *church* is also a bad translation. It should say to call for the elders of the assembly or congregation. The point is that the word that is translated as synagogue in Revelation and the word that is translated as church in James mean the same thing—an assembly or congregation of anyone, Jew, Christian, or pagan. But don't take my word for it, look it up yourself.

Those who have used these Scriptures to justify anti-Semitism should reconsider their understanding of these Scriptures and repent of their anti-Semitism. Whoever this group is, Jews or pretend Jews, Jesus said, *"Father, forgive them, for they do not know what they do"* (Luke 23:34).

The Promise (verses 10-11)

Jesus gives a final word of hope to the congregation at Smyrna in the form of a promise. But first He encourages them to overcome their fears, because there is more persecution ahead for them. Our Lord's words to His followers who are being persecuted are still timely for us today: *"And do not fear those who kill the body but cannot kill the soul. But rather fear Him who is able to destroy both the soul and body in hell"* (Matt. 10:28).

Some from the congregation at Smyrna will be put in prison, some tortured, and some martyred. This is not good news. None of us likes to suffer, and believers have had their share. Unfortunately, there is more to come. But the good news is that it will be over soon. Jesus says it will last ten days, meaning a short period of time.

Most of us can endure hardship if we can "see the light at the end of the tunnel." This gives us hope that our situation is going to get better. Jesus gives Smyrna that hope—their suffering will be over soon. While we don't know what *soon* means in terms of time, sooner is better than later.

Jesus identifies the real enemy—the devil. In this instance, satan is working through the persecutors to slander the believers. It is a test of their faith, as it is easy to be a believer when there are no tests, no trials, and no tribulation. The fact that satan is working so hard to destroy the believing community in Smyrna is a real testimony to their lives. They are making a difference. Otherwise, satan would not be attacking them with such fierce determination. This is why we can rejoice when we are *"persecuted for righteousness' sake"* (Matt. 5:10).

It is better to live for God and suffer, if need be, than live for ourselves in ease. If we can get this perspective, we can rejoice when we are suffering for righteous reasons. Jesus said it this way:

> Blessed are you when they revile and persecute you, and say all kinds of evil against you falsely for My sake. Rejoice and be exceedingly glad, for great is your reward in heaven, for so they persecuted the prophets who were before you (Matthew 5:11-12).

These suffering saints have a promise from the Lord. He says that those who overcome will be given the crown of life and will not be hurt by the second death. These are two ways of saying the same thing. By using the phrase *"crown of life"* (Rev. 2:10), Jesus is speaking in terms the believers can relate to, since every day they see the highest point in Smyrna referred to as the "Crown of Smyrna." Whereas the Crown of Smyrna will eventually be nothing but ruins (as it is today), the crown of life lasts forever. Perhaps this is what the Lord means by their suffering lasting only a short time.

The Lord is promising them that He will raise them from the dead as He was raised from the dead, that they will reign with Him on the earth, and that they will live with Him in eternity in a New Jerusalem where there is no suffering. The same promise is for God's people today.

As we learn later in John's apocalyptic vision:

> And I saw thrones, and they sat on them, and judgment was committed to them. Then I saw the souls of those who had been beheaded for their witness to Jesus and for the word of God, who had not worshiped the beast or his image, and had not received his mark on their foreheads or on their hands. And they lived and reigned with Christ [Messiah] for a thousand years. But the rest of the dead did not live again until the thousand years were finished.

This is the first resurrection. Blessed and holy is he who has part in the first resurrection. Over such the second death has no power, but they shall be priests of God and of Christ [Messiah], and shall reign with Him a thousand years (Revelation 20:4-6).

In one final vision, John writes:

Now I saw a new heaven and a new earth, for the first heaven and the first earth had passed away. Also there was no more sea. Then I, John, saw the holy city, New Jerusalem, coming down out of heaven from God, prepared as a bride adorned for her husband. And I heard a loud voice from heaven saying, "Behold, the tabernacle of God is with men, and He will dwell with them, and they shall be His people. God Himself will be with them and be their God. And God will wipe away every tear from their eyes; there shall be no more death, nor sorrow, nor crying. There shall be no more pain, for the former things have passed away."

Then He who sat on the throne said, "Behold, I will make all things new." And He said to me, "Write, for these words are true and faithful." And He said to me, "It is done! I am the Alpha and the Omega, the Beginning and the End. I will give of the fountain of the water of life freely to him who thirsts. He who overcomes shall inherit all things, and I will be his God and he shall be My son. But the cowardly, unbelieving, abominable, murderers, sexual immoral, sorcerers, idolaters, and all liars shall have their part in the lake which burns with fire and brimstone, which is the second death" (Revelation 21:1-8).

Paul's words to the congregation in Rome have given comfort to suffering believers for centuries. May they comfort us as well:

> *Who shall separate us from the love of Christ [Messiah]? Shall tribulation, or distress, or persecution, or famine, or nakedness, or peril, or sword? As it is written: "For Your sake we are killed all day long; we are accounted as sheep for the slaughter."*

> *Yet in all these things we are more than conquerors through Him who loved us. For I am persuaded that neither death nor life, nor angels nor principalities nor powers, nor things present nor things to come, nor height nor depth, nor any other created thing, shall be able to separate us from the love of God which is in Christ Jesus [Messiah Yeshua] our Lord* (Romans 8:35-39).

If the Lord's message to Smyrna applies to your organization, your ministry, or your life, let us find comfort in the words of Jesus:

> *Blessed are those who are persecuted for righteousness' sake, for theirs is the kingdom of heaven. Blessed are you when they revile and persecute you, and say all kinds of evil against you falsely for My sake. Rejoice and be exceedingly glad, for great is your reward in heaven, for so they persecuted the prophets who were before you* (Matthew 5:10-12).

He who has an ear, let him hear.

Review Questions

1. Write a summary of what you have learned in this lesson. Write the summary in clear concise words as if you are going to present it to another person.

2. Write an explanation of how you can apply what you have learned in this lesson to your life.

3. Share what you have learned with your family, friends, and members of your study group.

Endnote

1. Brent Walters, *Ante-Nicene Christianity: The First Three Centuries* (San Jose, CA: Ante-Nicene Archive, 1993), 52-53.

Chapter 8

The Letter to Pergamos

REVELATION REVIEW

WE owe so much to the believers at Smyrna. When this life is over, we will meet our brothers and sisters from Smyrna who endured persecution and even martyrdom for the sake of the Lord and for us who would become believers many centuries later. May we be counted worthy of their ultimate sacrifice on our behalf. And may God forgive us for taking for granted the blessings they made possible for us, and forgive us for preaching an "easy believism," "feel good," "entertainment" Gospel message.

Because they were suffering persecution and death for their faith, the Lord greeted them as the One who had overcome death. This is why He promised the overcomers that they would not be hurt by the second death. God would resurrect them and give them the crown of life.

It is noteworthy that the Lord had no rebuke for the believers at Smyrna. This is also true for the congregation at Philadelphia. There is an important lesson here for us. The believers at Smyrna were facing great persecution and poverty. Like the name of their city, their life as a new community of faith in a pagan town was bittersweet. While the

Lord had strong words of warning to the more prosperous congregations, He had only words of encouragement for the believers at Smyrna. What does this mean to us?

When we study the history of revivals and great awakenings among God's people, we discover that great moves of God happened in times of severe persecution. They never happened when God's people were comfortable. This is the lesson for us to learn. We should have serious concern when Christianity becomes popular, because the message of the cross will never be popular with secular culture or with the masses.

As a modern example, consider the great move of God in China. When the Gospel message first came to China, believers suffered tremendously. They were persecuted, imprisoned, and martyred. While China today is certainly more open to freedom of religion, official government-approved churches (congregations) are still controlled by the government. As long as these congregations don't become too popular so that they threaten the government, they have relative freedom of worship. However, believers who meet in house churches (congregations) are often persecuted by the authorities. Yet, in spite of this persecution, or perhaps because of it, Christianity in China has grown faster than in any other part of the world.

It is certainly not popular to be a Christian in China. Christianity is not part of the Chinese culture and is often considered a Western religion and unwanted influence and intrusion. Yet, because of the huge population of China, and due to the commitment of Chinese believers, there are more Christians in China than in America. While this may be hard to believe, China is becoming more Christian and America more pagan. I think this is happening right before our eyes as God is moving the center of Christianity from the West to the East. What will it take for God to bring a revival of holiness and the fear of the Lord to American believers?

The Lord commended the believers for their works, for enduring tribulation, for their faithfulness even when it meant financial loss, and reminded them that He knew who was persecuting them. In other words, in due time, He would avenge them. As America becomes more and more anti-Judeo-Christian, we will see great persecution of Jews and Christians. Any discerning believer should see this happening. As this hatred of Jews and Christians becomes more aggressive and apparent, may the Lord be able to say the same words to us that He did to the believers at Smyrna.

BACKGROUND

Before reading the Lord's letter to the believers at Pergamos, let's learn what life was like in that ancient city. After taking John's letter to be read at Smyrna, the courier continued on the Roman postal road to Pergamos, also spelled Pergamum, which was about 50 miles north of Smyrna and about 15 miles inland.

The name *Pergamos* means "citadel, elevated, or exalted," and characterized this city which sat on top of a thousand-foot hill that overlooked the surrounding countryside. It was a natural fortress. Pergamos was also exalted as the chief religious center in the province, with many magnificent temples to different gods and goddesses. Scholars believe the population of Pergamos when John wrote his prophetic message was about 150,000.

When Alexander the Great died, one of his generals, Lysimachus, conquered the area of Pergamos and entrusted a large fortune to Philetaerus, who was one of his officers. When Lysimachus was killed in battle, Philetaerus used the wealth entrusted to him to build Pergamos into an independent Greek kingdom. When he died, his successors, known as the Attalid dynasty, greatly expanded the Kingdom of Pergamos, ruling over it for five generations. This covered the period of time from 263-133 B.C. When Attalus III died in 133 B.C., he gave the Kingdom of Pergamos to the Roman government. At this time, Pergamos was incorporated into the Roman province of Asia Minor and was its chief city and official capital, with a local Roman proconsul.

Pergamos was famous for its huge library, which rivaled the larger one in Alexandria, Egypt. The library housed about 200,000 volumes, making Pergamos a great learning center for the whole region, and attracting visitors from far and wide.

During this time, papyrus was the main material for writing, and Alexandria controlled the papyrus market. Due to their rivalry, Alexandria stopped shipping papyrus to the library at Pergamos. As a result, Pergamos developed parchment (made from animal skins) as a new material for writing. In fact the word *parchment* means "belonging to or of Pergamos." However, Alexandria eventually won the rivalry when in 41 B.C. Mark Antony plundered the library and gave the books to Cleopatra.

Along with its university and medical center, Pergamos had one of the most impressive theaters of the ancient world. It was the steepest theater of its day, being situated on the side of the hill. It had a seating capacity of 10,000 people. Because of its location, the acoustics were so good that people could not only clearly hear the performers, they also had a magnificent view of the surrounding countryside.

The modern city of Bergama is located at the ruins of ancient Pergamos. The city has a population of 75,000-100,000 and is known for its high-quality Bergama carpets. The city has 15 mosques and a professing Christian community. Its main archaeological site is the Bergama Archaeological Museum, containing a replica of the altar to Zeus which is in the Pergamon Museum in Berlin.

TO THE CONGREGATION AT PERGAMOS
(REVELATION 2:12-17)

Greeting (verse 12)

With this brief background, let's read the Lord's prophetic letter to the believers at Pergamos.

The Son of Man greets the believers at Pergamos in the way that addresses their situation. He also refers to Himself in a way that relates back to His glorious revelation given to John in Revelation 1:16. He says He *"has the sharp two-edged sword"* (Rev. 2:12).

What does this symbol mean? We discussed the different kinds of swords in Chapter 5. The Romans developed a sword that had a revolutionary design which enabled the Roman soldier to attack his enemy with a slicing motion from either side of the sword. It was a sharp, two-edged sword.

In Pergamos, the Roman proconsul had such a sword. He also had what was called "the right of the sword." This means that he had the authority to use his sword to execute judgment as he thought necessary.

Unfortunately, the believers at Pergamos lived under the threat of "the right of the sword." Jesus used this situation to remind them that He too had a sword that was more powerful than the one used by the Roman official. Like the Roman proconsul, He too had "the right of the sword." And His right came from a higher authority than Rome. His "right of the sword" came from His Father in Heaven. His sword is the creative power of His spoken Word.

This is the same truth that Jesus revealed to us when He stood before Pilate. When Jesus would not defend Himself, Pilate said to Him, *"Do You not know that I have the power to crucify You, and power to release You?"* (John 19:10). Jesus responded, *"You could have no power at all against Me unless it had been given you from above..."* (John 19:11).

Like Pilate, the Roman proconsul at Pergamos thought that he was the ultimate authority because he had "the right of the sword." Being only human, this situation would certainly frighten and intimidate the believers. So Jesus reminds them that He has the ultimate authority over life and death by the power of His spoken Word.

In Revelation 1:16, John says that Jesus' words are like a sharp two-edged sword coming out of His mouth. When the New Testament talks about God's Word coming out of His mouth, it uses the Greek word *rhema*. As one example, Jesus said, *"Man shall not live by bread alone, but by every word* [rhema] *that proceeds from the mouth of God"* (Matt. 4:4).

Since God's Words are in Him and part of His being, they have His life in them. When He speaks, His Words come out of Him with His life in them to perform what He speaks. This is how God can speak something out of nothing. His life is in His spoken Words.

When the Son of Man speaks, His Words are more powerful than a Roman sword. The sword used by the Roman proconsul can kill the believers but the Sword of the Lord can destroy Rome. The Sword of the Spirit proceeding out of the mouth of the Son of Man can destroy nations and all the enemies of God and His people.

We learn later in Revelation that when the Lord returns, He destroys the nations with His spoken word, *"Now out of His mouth goes a sharp sword, that with it He should strike the nations"* (Rev. 19:15). John says that those who survive the final battle against the Lord are killed with the sword which proceeded from the mouth of Him who sat on the throne (see Rev. 19:21).

While governments may persecute God's people even to the point of martyrdom, in God's time He will avenge His people by the two-edged sword of His spoken Word. We do not have to fear those who only have a physical sword. The Lord will destroy our enemies. Victory is certain. As He did with Lazarus, Jesus will raise us from the dead by the power of His spoken Word. We will hear His voice and live (see John 5:24-29). We will sit with Him on thrones and judge those who persecuted us (see Rev. 20:4).

The Commendation (verse 13)

Jesus reassures the congregation at Pergamos that He knows their works and He knows that they live in a city where satan's throne is and where satan dwells. WOW! They live where satan lives and has his throne. I think I would move if I lived there. What was the situation at Pergamos that would have Jesus make such startling statements?

Pergamos was the pagan religious capital of Asia Minor. Now I know I would move. How about you? The city was filled with temples, statues, and altars devoted to idol worship and the immoral festivals associated with idolatry that were part of the Pergamos way of life. There were three aspects of pagan worship that characterized the city.

First, Pergamos was the transplanted capital of Babylonian sun worship. You see, when the Medo-Persians defeated the Babylonians in 536 B.C., many of the Babylonian priests fled to Asia Minor and established their spiritual center at Pergamos. Later, the Attalid dynasty of kings accepted the role as the political and spiritual heirs and representatives of Babylonian sun worship instituted by Nimrod.

When Attalus III handed over his kingdom to Rome, the religious headship of Babylonian sun worship was passed to Rome. When Julius Caesar became the absolute ruler, he claimed to be a descendant of the gods, and embraced both the political and religious role of king-priest of the old Babylonian religion. Thus Rome succeeded Pergamos as the new superpower religious heir to Babylonian sun worship. The Roman emperor was the head of both the Roman government and the Roman version of the old Babylonian religion.

When Constantine became the Roman emperor, he needed to unite the empire under one religion. Seeing how many of his subjects were embracing Christianity, he made cosmetic changes to Babylonian sun worship and redefined Christianity into a Greco-Roman religion. His purpose was to blend them into one religion that would be acceptable to his subjects.

Constantine was very successful in his efforts. To him and the pagan sun worshipers of his empire, the sun god of Babylonia and the Sun of Righteousness were one and the same. Like the city of Pergamos, the old religion of Babylonia was set on high, elevated, and exalted under the guise of Christianity as the religion of the empire. Rome became the citadel of the newly redefined Christian religion.

The second aspect of pagan worship that characterized the city was the imperial cult worship. Pergamos was the first city in the Roman province to institute emperor worship. The city built a temple to Augustus in 29 B.C. Later they built temples to the Emperors Trajan and Hadrian. Pergamos became known as the "City of Three Temples," where the emperors were worshiped as gods.

A third aspect of worship at Pergamos that made it the religious capital of the province were the magnificent temples and altars built to four great gods of paganism—Zeus, Athena, Dionysus, and Asclepius.

In Greek religion and mythology, Zeus was the supreme god. As the king of the gods, Zeus was worshiped as god and lord and savior of almost every aspect of life. Because Zeus was the "high god of the gods," the altar dedicated to him was the most spectacular structure at Pergamos. Built high up on the hill overlooking the city, the throne-like altar was one of the ancient wonders of the world. It was shaped like a horseshoe, 100 feet long on both sides and 40 feet high. The altar was made with characters showing Zeus defeating snake-like giants.

From this high position, the altar depicted him as "Zeus the Savior" overlooking the city. In the 1870s, German engineer Carl Humann discovered the altar. In 1871 the altar was taken to Germany where it is now on exhibit at the Pergamon Museum in Berlin. The Romans equated Zeus with their own supreme god, Jupiter.

Athena was the patron goddess of Athens. Greek mythology tells how her "father" Zeus gave birth to her. Zeus was told that one of his children would overthrow him. So whenever his wife, Metis, bore a child, Zeus ate the child. Eventually, Zeus got smart and ate Metis to prevent her from having any more children.

Unknown to Zeus, Metis was already pregnant with Athena. Much like mothers who knit clothes for their yet-to-be-born babies, Metis made a robe and helmet for Athena. When Metis hammered on the helmet, Zeus cried out in great pain, as it gave him a headache. (Serves him right, don't you think?) When the time came for Athena to be born, she burst forth from Zeus' head fully grown and wearing the robe and helmet her mother made her.

Athena was the favorite daughter of Zeus. She was worshiped as the patron goddess of different areas of life, including wisdom, war, trade skills and crafts, and the making of weapons. People involved in trades joined the Athena Union. They sacrificed to her and sought her help in their work. She was considered by many as the protector of the city. In Greek mythology, Athena was a virgin and given the title *Athena Parthenos,* meaning, *Athena the Virgin.* The Parthenon in Athens was built to worship her. Dionysus, a son of Zeus, was the god of wine, drunken revelry, debauchery, and sexual gratification. Need I say more? According to Greek mythology, Dionysus discovered the art of winemaking. He then traveled to different lands, teaching his worshipers how to cultivate the vine to make the best wine. Dionysus worshipers took wine tasting to a new level.

Many festivals were held in honor of Dionysus, and for good reason. It gave people an excuse to get drunk and indulge in every imaginable form of sexual perversion. Worshipers sought union with Dionysus, who would empower them with the ability to experience ecstasy. We don't need much imagination to figure out what the worshipers did at the temple devoted to Dionysus.

Asclepius was the god of healing. He was the patron god of Pergamos and his likeness appeared on their coins. Much like major medical centers today, people would come from far and wide to the temple in Pergamos, seeking healing. There was a large medical center associated with the temple, and many "healing priests" who served Asclepius.

Since the symbol for Asclepius was the serpent, the temple dedicated to him had temple snakes that were considered the embodiment of Asclepius. These were not poisonous snakes, but were "medical snakes" that helped to heal people. Here is how it worked. The sick worshipers were allowed to sleep in the temple at night. If a "medical snake" happened to touch them, it was as if Asclepius had touched them, and they would be healed.

Of course, the priests serving the healing snake god made sure that only those people that they themselves could help had the blessing of spending the night with the snakes. So they inspected the poor sufferers, or as we would say, made them take a medical exam, before admitting them to the temple (hospital).

We see that Pergamos had everything in the way of pagan worship opportunities. With Zeus overlooking the city, there was nothing to worry about. He was your lord and savior. If you were so inclined, you could be part of the old Babylonian worship of the sun. You could even choose which emperor you wanted to worship. You could join the Augustine denomination, the Trajan denomination, or the Hadrian denomination. Or if you were really religious, you could join all three.

And if you were a member of a trade guild (union) you were blessed with a temple to Athena. Of course to join the guild, you had to worship Athena by making sacrifices to her, and eating meat that was left over from the sacrifices, and also desire to have union with her.

If you were a "Pergamos, pagan, party person," the temple to Dionysus was open 24 hours a day. There was no limit to your revelry, and you did not need a designated driver, as you could pass out at the temple and the temple prostitutes would take care of you.

If you got sick, there was the snake god to heal you. It helped to know one of the priests personally; otherwise, you might not get admitted. There were never enough snakes to go around, so not everyone got healed.

The citizens at Pergamos had many festivals and everyday worship activities devoted to their different gods. There was something for everyone. Their way to worship their gods was to bow down before the gods while making a sacrifice, then eat the meat left over as a form of worship, and participate in the various temple rituals and activities that embodied the nature and character of the gods. Living right in the middle of all of this was a small group of believers who received a prophetic message from the Son of Man.

The Lord commended these courageous believers because they held fast to His Name and did not deny their faith. While under great stress and constant fear for their lives, they were loyal and faithful to the Lord. They acknowledged the God of Abraham, Isaac, and Jacob, not the Babylonian sun god, as the One True God; and Jesus, not Zeus, as Savior and Lord. They did not compromise their beliefs in order to prosper, or to make business contacts and be accepted by the community at large. They did not water down their teachings to be popular, politically correct, or socially acceptable.

They were not "seeker-friendly," because who in his right mind in Pergamos would want to join their community? They did not give in to peer pressure. They refused to "fix their sandals" at the altars to the emperors. They would not bow before the pagan deities or participate in the idolatry and immorality which characterized the city.

They could not attend the civic activities and sporting events because they were dedicated to the gods. Social contact outside of their own activities was difficult, as most of it was related to the gods. It was difficult for them to get good jobs because they had to join a local trade guild which was dedicated to Athena. They did not intermarry with nonbelievers. It was very difficult for them to live and function in Pergamos.

These brave believers maintained a faithful witness even though one of them was martyred. We don't know anything about Antipas other than what is said about him in this commendation. Yet, his courage was an example and encouragement to the believers to remain strong and faithful in their commitment to the Lord, as witness to the city.

While satan thought he would intimidate the believers by putting Antipas to death, the result was just the opposite. They were even more determined in their faith. It has been this way throughout the ages. The congregation of the Lord has been built on the blood of its martyrs.

While demonic-inspired leaders and dictators think that they can destroy the work of God through murder, fear, and intimidation, the results are always just the opposite. When unbelievers see the faith and courage of believers, even to the point of death, they are attracted to such people and the God they serve. However, compromise has the opposite results. Unbelievers are not attracted to people who compromise their beliefs and lifestyle for whatever purpose.

Yet there were some in the congregation at Pergamos who were compromising their faith and way of life. Their actions were threatening the integrity and witness of the community, and brought about a rebuke and warning from the Lord.

The Rebuke (verses 14-16)

Jesus reprimands this steadfast congregation because they were tolerating some among them who accepted the doctrine of Balaam and the Nicolaitans. What was this doctrine that Jesus said He hated?

Students of the Bible remember the story of Balaam in the Hebrew Scriptures as recorded in Numbers 22-31. The Moabite King Balak was afraid of the Israelites. He sent for Balaam, a prophet for hire, to curse them. Yet each time Balaam opened his mouth to curse them, God made him speak blessings instead.

King Balak offered Balaam more money, thinking this would cause him to finally curse the Israelites. But the offer of money didn't work. Balaam kept blessing the people he was supposed to curse.

After four tries, and being rebuked by his own donkey, Balaam realized that God was not going to let him curse the Israelites. Balaam figured out a way to indirectly curse them. He counseled King Balak to tempt the Israelite men by inviting them to participate in their pagan worship and festivals. The idolatry included offering sacrifices to the Moabite gods, eating the remainder of the sacrifices as a form of worship, and committing immorality with the Moabite women as part of the worship.

The Book of Numbers tells us:

> *Now Israel remained in Acacia Grove, and the people began to commit harlotry with the women of Moab. They invited the people to the sacrifices of their gods, and the people ate and bowed down to their gods* (Numbers 25:1-2).

The story goes on to tell us that the Lord was angry with His own people and allowed a plague against those who participated.

We learn from this story that the doctrine of Balaam was the teaching that God's people could mix and mingle with the heathen in their idolatrous worship which, in Bible times, always led to immorality, intermarriage, and compromise in faith and lifestyle. Eating food offered to idols was not the issue if it was bought in the marketplace. The issue was participating in the heathen worship, festivities, and prayers, which included eating the food that had been offered to the idols.

The Nicolaitans were professing believers in the congregation who accepted, taught, and practiced the doctrine of Balaam. Unless they repented, they would influence the rest of the believers to accept their teaching and compromise their faith and witness. The Son of Man warned that if they did not repent, He would fight against them Himself with the sword of His mouth.

Unfortunately, there are professing Christian leaders and believers today who accept and practice the doctrine of Balaam and the Nicolaitans. Some Christian leaders, like Balaam, are "preachers-for-hire" who only preach what the people want to hear. They have a watered down "feel good" message that fits well with our carnal culture. They entertain the crowd but rarely mention sin and holiness. They certainly don't call people to repent of their worldly ways and live godly lives.

People pay preachers good money to tell them what they want to hear. The New Testament warns against these ministers who tickle the people's ears. Peter writes, *"They have forsaken the right way and gone astray, following the way of Balaam the son of Beor, who loved the wages of unrighteousness"* (2 Pet. 2:15).

Jude adds, *"Woe to them! For they have gone in the way of Cain, have run greedily in the error of Balaam for profit, and perished in the rebellion of Korah"* (Jude 11).

Paul's instructions to Timothy are a reminder to every minister:

> *Preach the word! Be ready in season and out of season. Convince, rebuke, exhort, with all longsuffering and teaching. For the time will come when they will not endure sound doctrine, but according to their own desires, because they have itching ears, they will heap up for themselves teachers; and they will turn their ears away from the truth, and be turned aside to fables* (2 Timothy 4:2-4).

Believers today have the same challenges as those at Pergamos. While we may not worship physical idols, the attitudes, pleasures, pressures, distractions, greed, and ways of the world are a constant temptation to compromise our beliefs, our faith message, our moral standards, and our lifestyle in order to be accepted and prosper in our anti-God world system.

As America becomes more and more like Pergamos, let us turn away from the doctrine of Balaam and the Nicolaitans. May we not compromise our faith and witness for the sake of family, riches and honor, advancement, personal gain, acceptance, intimidation and fear of government, or any other worldly concern. Let us be faithful and steadfast like the believers at Pergamos.

May we take to heart Paul's words which are so relevant to our world today:

> *I beseech you therefore, brethren, by the mercies of God, that you present your bodies a living sacrifice, holy, acceptable to God, which is your reasonable service. And do not be conformed to this world, but be transformed by the renewing of your mind, that you may prove what is that good and acceptable and perfect will of God* (Romans 12:1-2).

The Promise (verse 17)

To those who hear His voice and repent, the Lord makes three wonderful promises. First He says He will give them the hidden manna to eat, which is a promise of spiritual food for the soul and eternal life (see Rev. 2:17).

Jesus is referring to the supernatural provision of manna that God gave to the Hebrews every morning for the 40 years they were wandering in the wilderness (see Exod. 16). It was sweet bread from Heaven that replaced the garlic and onions of Egypt. The manna was their nourishment that sustained them.

When the Hebrews built the tabernacle of Moses, God instructed them to place a pot of the manna in the Ark of the Covenant as a reminder of how He provided for them (see Exod. 16:31-35).

When Jesus was ministering on the earth, He presented Himself as the Living Bread of God who came from Heaven with the supernatural, sweet Word of God to feed our hungry souls. John records the miracle of Jesus feeding the 5,000 men plus women and children by multiplying the five loaves of bread. Jesus claimed to be the true bread of God who came down from Heaven with spiritual food (see John 6).

Jesus ended His sermon with these words:

As the living Father sent Me, and I live because of the Father, so he who feeds on Me will live because of Me. This is the bread which came down from heaven—not as your fathers ate the manna, and are dead. He who eats this bread will live forever (John 6:57-58).

Second, Jesus promises the congregation at Pergamos a white stone. In ancient times, stones had various uses. There were stones of remembrance, stones that were used like an admission ticket to an event, stones as rewards for victors in games, and stones exchanged between friends. In a court of law, those found not guilty were given a white stone, while those found guilty were given a black stone.

White stones were used by the government to write official decrees and announcements. With all the religious events in Pergamos, it was likely that white stones were often distributed to citizens and worshipers as a way of making important announcements about festivals or political events. Trade guilds would have issued white stones with the person's name, inviting them to special meetings and banquets to honor Athena. Except for those who held to the doctrine of Balaam and the Nicolaitans, the believers didn't get white stone invitations bearing their names.

Jesus promised His overcomers a white stone invitation to an event much greater than any pagan banquet in Pergamos. His invitation was to the Messiah's banquet at His coming. John was told to write these words: *"Blessed are those who are called to the marriage supper of the Lamb"* (Rev. 19:9).

Those who overcome will be given a white stone with their name showing that the court of Heaven has found them not guilty of their sins because Jesus accepted the black stone of judgment for them on the cross. God has forgiven our sins to be remembered no more. He has cast them into the sea of forgetfulness. He has separated us from our sins as far as the east is from the west.

The Lord said He will give us a new name written on the stone that no one knows but the one who receives it. In the Bible, a person's name indicated the nature and character of the person. The new name the Lord will write on the white stone represents our own personal inheritance in Heaven. While we alone know what our relationship with God was like on the earth, we will be known by our new name, which is God's own glory emanating out of us throughout eternity.

John boldly declares, *"They shall see His face, and His name shall be on their foreheads"* (Rev. 22:4).

If the Lord's message to Pergamos applies to your organization, your ministry, or your life, let us repent and do what He says. Let us heed the words of Paul, who reminds us:

> *For the grace of God that brings salvation has appeared to all men, teaching us that, denying ungodliness and worlds lusts, we should live soberly, righteously, and godly in the present age, looking for the blessed hope and glorious appearing of our great God and Savior Jesus Christ* [Yeshua the Messiah]... (Titus 2:11-13).

He who has an ear, let him hear.

Review Questions

1. Write a summary of what you have learned in this lesson. Write the summary in clear concise words as if you are going to present it to another person.

2. Write an explanation of how you can apply what you have learned in this lesson to your life.

3. Share what you have learned with your family, friends, and members of your study group.

Chapter 9

The Letter to Thyatira

REVELATION REVIEW

IF you were a pagan party person, Pergamos was just the place for you. Because Pergamos was the heart of imperial cult worship and the worship of Zeus, Jesus called it the seat of satan. Pergamos was the pagan religious capital of Western Asia and was filled with temples and altars to the gods and goddesses of the Greco-Roman world.

While ancient Babylon was conquered politically and militarily by subsequent empires, Babylonian sun worship survived and even flourished. For a time, Pergamos became the center of this ancient religion that would later influence the world through Constantine. To Westerners who have a Judeo-Christian heritage, it is hard to believe that there are people in the modern world who still worship the sun. There are. On a ministry trip to India, I saw many early risers worshiping the sun.

Also, if you were really into emperor worship, you could get your fill of it at Pergamos. No other city in Asia Minor was as zealous in paying homage to the emperors as Pergamos. It was the center of imperial cult worship, with temples built to Augustus, Trajan, and Hadrian. In addition to everyday worship of the emperors, Rome held special festive days in which the emperors were honored. All the citizens were publicly required to bow before the statue or altar of the emperor, make a sacrifice, and proclaim, "Caesar is Lord." The local Roman proconsul had the "right of the sword" to enforce this show of loyalty to the empire.

Then there were the temples built to the Greek deities of Zeus, Athena, Dionysus, and Asklepois. Since Zeus was considered the "god of gods" in Greek mythology, Pergamos was a very important center of pagan worship. Trade guilds were dedicated to these gods and goddesses. In order to have a job or be accepted in the community, you had to express your devotion to these false deities. It was very difficult for believers to survive in Pergamos.

It is truly remarkable that a local congregation survived at Pergamos. The Lord commended some for their faith and steadfastness. However, given the circumstances, we shouldn't be surprised that there were others in the congregation who taught that they could compromise to keep their jobs, not to mention their lives. The Lord promised spiritual blessings to those who overcame, but warned the compromisers that He had the right of the Sword of the Spirit which He would use against them.

This is such a relevant message for us today. Because America was birthed with a Judeo-Christian heritage, it has been easy to be a believer in America. Until recently, believers were favored in every area of American life. Unfortunately, this is rapidly changing. Unbelievers are now favored by the elite in all areas of American life, while believers are being ridiculed and excluded from many positions and opportunities. Already, we see Christian leaders and ordinary believers compromising in order to have favor with the secular anti-God establishment. While God will bless believers who are faithful to Him, He will judge those who compromise His Word and His moral standards.

With this review, let's now learn about life in Thyatira as background to the Lord's letter to the believers in this Greco-Roman city. As with the other towns of John's revelation, the Lord had planted a little colony of Heaven right in the midst of this ancient pagan city.

BACKGROUND

After delivering the Lord's prophetic letter to the believers at Pergamos, the courier traveled about 40 miles southeast to Thyatira. Thyatira was located about 42 miles inland from the Aegean Sea.

As with other towns and cities in Asia Minor, when Alexander defeated the Persian Empire, one of his successors, Seleucus, rebuilt Thyatira. It originally served as a military outpost from which it got its name, which meant the "citadel, castle or stronghold of Thya."

Thyatira was located on the main Roman postal route, as were each of the other seven cities with a community of believers. Historically, Thyatira was not a large, influential city. However, the city became an important commercial center because it had the natural resources and skilled craftsman to make the much sought after purple dye. The color was probably scarlet, but in ancient times, people used the word *purple* to refer to various color shades of red. Unlike the purple dye made from snails, the dye of Thyatira was made from a madder-root plant, and is now called "Turkey red." We learn in the Bible that Lydia was a seller of purple from Thyatira. She was living in Philippi when she heard Paul preach the Gospel. Lydia was a worshiper of the One True God. When she heard Paul's message, she became a believer, was baptized in the river on Shabbat, and gave hospitality to Paul and Silas. She was apparently Paul's first convert in what would be considered Europe, and the congregation of new believers met in her home. (See Acts 16:11-15.)

We don't know who first shared the Gospel in Thyatira or when the first congregation was established. But we do know that Christianity took root in the city. The growth and influence of the congregation was such that they had a bishop who attended the Council of Nicea in A.D. 325 and the Council of Ephesus in A.D. 431.

Thyatira was known for its many trade guilds. Today we might think of Thyatira as a factory, blue-collar, union town. Archaeologists have discovered many coins and inscriptions mentioning different trade guilds, such as dyers, wool, linen, leather and bronze, potters, tanners and bakers. Each industry had its own trade guild.

The norm in ancient times was that the trade guilds acknowledged a certain deity. The gods and goddesses had their origins in Babylon. When Babylon was conquered by the Medo-Persians, the conquerors embraced the old Babylonian deities and simply changed their names to be part of the pantheon of the gods and goddesses worshiped by the conquerors.

When Alexander conquered the Persians, the gods and goddesses of Greek mythology became the primary deities worshiped by the pagan world. They would later be "made over" as Roman deities when Rome became the new world power. This was the situation in Thyatira and with the entire Mediterranean world when John sent his prophetic messages to the seven congregations.

Like a "closed shop" union town of today, people had to join the guilds in order to get a job. When the guild members assembled, the normal order of business was to worship their particular deity and seek its blessings. The way they did this was to sacrifice to the deity and then eat the remainder of the sacrifice. The reason for doing this was not only to have the food to eat; eating the sacrificial offering was part of the worship. It showed their covenant union with the gods and goddesses they worshiped. It was the guild's communal feast (communion meal) to their patron deity. As with all idol worship, drunkenness and immorality often accompanied the worship.

In order to have a job and advance socially or any other way in Thyatira, a craftsman had to belong to the guild of his trade. For believers, this meant participating in the worship by eating the sacrifices and joining in the unholy revelry. Someone in the congregation taught that it was OK for the believers to participate. This was the situation facing the believers that prompted the Son of Man to send them a prophetic letter.

When Rome established its authority in the region, Thyatira became part of the Roman province of Asia Minor. The modern Turkish city of Akhisar is located at the site of the ruins of Thyatira. The main archaeological sites are fourth- through sixth-century public buildings. With this background, let's now see what the Lord had to say to the believers at Thyatira.

TO THE CONGREGATION AT THYATIRA
(REVELATION 2:18-29)

The Greeting (verse 18)

The Son of Man identifies Himself also as the Son of God. Some scholars say that Jesus never claimed to be the Son of God, but that His followers made this claim later in order to present Jesus as more than just a human being, prophet, teacher, and healer. In other words, they invented this teaching, but Jesus never claimed this for Himself.

It is important that we study the Bible for ourselves and not accept what people say, because every teacher has his or her own agenda. They will interpret the Bible in ways to support their agendas and then teach and write books to promote their views. So what does the Bible say? Is Jesus just a remarkable prophet and great teacher? Or does the New Testament present Jesus as the Son of God? The answer is clearly *yes!*

In reference to Jesus, the phrase "Son of God" or "Son" used alone but in relationship to God is found about 95 times in the New Testament. You can count them yourself. That should be enough to clarify the issue. But just in case one still thinks this phrase was an invention of His followers, Jesus Himself greets the congregation in Thyatira as the Son of God. People may not believe Jesus is the Son of God, but they cannot claim that He did not call Himself by this phrase. Furthermore, during the time of Jesus, mystical rabbis who were considered close to God were often referred to as "sons of God." So this was not a new and strange idea for John's readers. The difference is that Jesus is the unique Son of God in that He was God in human flesh.

We have learned that Jesus identified Himself differently to each congregation based on the particular problems and issues facing the community. This is the only time the phrase "Son of God" is found in the Book of Revelation. So what was going on at Thyatira that prompted Jesus to identify Himself in this way?

As with the other congregations to whom Jesus is writing, the citizens of Thyatira worshiped a number of different deities, but their chief god was Apollo. In Greek mythology, Apollo was a son of Zeus, who was the supreme god and father of gods. Apollo was worshiped throughout the ancient world as a "son of god," meaning "son of Zeus." Among other attributes, Apollo was identified as the "sun god" and was called the radiant, shining one. He had an oracle (priest or priestess) who spoke on his behalf to his worshipers. The Roman emperors took this title on themselves and claimed to be the human incarnation of Zeus.

When the trade guilds met, they worshiped Apollo. If his local oracle spoke, they believed they were hearing the voice of the son of god speaking to them.

With this knowledge, it should be obvious why Jesus identified Himself as the Son of God. Zeus was not the supreme god and deity. Apollo was not the son of god and certainly not *"the Sun of Righteousness...with healing in His wings"* (Mal. 4:2). *YHVH*, the God of Abraham, Isaac, and Jacob is the one and only true God, and Jesus is His Son. As the Son of God, Jesus was the oracle who spoke for God. Whoever heard His voice, heard the voice of the Son of God.

In the Hebrew Scriptures, the One True God spoke to His people and told them to listen to His voice. The most important statement of faith for the Jewish people is, *"Hear, O Israel: The* LORD *our God, the* LORD *is one"* (Deut. 6:4)!

As time passed, God spoke to His people through His oracles, the prophets. But 2,000 years ago, God began to speak to His people through His perfect oracle, His Son, who would be God's Word in human flesh. The writer of Hebrews explains:

> *God, who at various times and in various ways spoke in time past to the fathers by the prophets, has in these last days spoken to us by His Son, whom He has appointed heir of all things, through whom also He made the worlds* (Hebrews 1:1-2).

As the glorified and exalted Son of God and Son of Man, Jesus is described in the way John saw Him in Revelation 1:14-15. His eyes are like a flame of fire and His feet like fine brass. Of course, this is symbolic apocalyptic language and not to be understood literally.

The Hebrew Bible tells us that God sees everything, good and evil, and rewards the good and judges the evil. Of the many verses we could quote, consider the following:

> *For the eyes of the* LORD *run to and fro throughout the whole earth, to show Himself strong on behalf of those whose heart is loyal to Him...* (2 Chronicles 16:9).

Proverbs 15:3 reads, *"The eyes of the* LORD *are in every place, keeping watch on the evil and the good."*

As God's Son, the divine DNA of His Father is in Jesus, enabling Him to have the same nature, characteristics and abilities of His Father. As the Son of God, with eyes like a flame of fire, Jesus is able to see past the outward facades and pretenses of people and look right into their hearts. Like natural fire, the fire of God in His Son is able to purify and cleanse the motives of His people while burning up the evil works and intentions of those who oppose Him.

While God is a God of mercy, He is also a God who judges sin and, in His own time, crushes evil people under His feet. His judgments are not out of emotional fits of anger, but are righteous judgments based on His moral character.

Moses wrote of God, *"He is the Rock, His work is perfect; for all His ways are justice, a God of truth and without injustice; righteous and upright* [just] *is He"* (Deut. 32:4).

Ecclesiastes 12:14 warns us, *"For God will bring every work into judgment, including every secret thing, whether good or evil."*

King David spoke these words about the righteous judgments of God:

> *The righteous shall rejoice when he sees the vengeance; He shall wash his feet in the blood of the wicked, so that men will say, "Surely there is a reward for the righteous; surely He is God who judges the earth"* (Psalms 58:10-11).

As the Son of God, Jesus executes the judgments of God on the earth. This is the meaning of the symbolic description of His feet—they are like fine brass (an alloy of copper with zinc), or burnished bronze (an alloy of copper with tin). These metals are a symbol of God's righteous judgments. Jesus is warning His people that He will judge (put under His feet) the evil in the congregation at Thyatira.

The Commendation (verse 19)

Because the Lord is gracious, He takes every opportunity to speak a positive word of encouragement for His people before pointing out their failures. He wants them to realize that He knows (is aware of) and is pleased with the good He sees in them. To the believers at Thyatira, He commends them for the following praiseworthy aspects of their congregational life:

1. Their works

2. Their love

3. Their service

4. Their faith

5. Their patience

6. Their spiritual progress

Wow! This is quite a commendation. This is a very active, loving congregation that is full of faith, as evidenced by their works of loving-kindness, their patience to endure in difficult circumstances, and their physical and spiritual growth.

The congregation at Thyatira had a lot going for it. There was a lot of spiritual life and vitality. In modern words, we might say this was a growing congregation with a place for everyone to get involved in the various ministries of the congregation. Most of us would be blessed to be part of this congregation. We would probably also be blessed if the Lord commended us personally the way He did the believers at Thyatira.

Yet, in spite of all the good things, the Lord sees a problem that is threatening the life and witness of the congregation. What was it that troubled the Lord about this otherwise healthy congregation?

The Rebuke (verses 20-25)

The Lord chastises them because they allowed a false prophetess identified as Jezebel to teach that it was acceptable for them to compromise and corrupt themselves by participating in the idolatry and immorality at the meetings of the guild. This was a common problem throughout the Mediterranean world facing the believers in the first few centuries. It was the same issue the Lord had with the congregation at Pergamos.

Of course the woman's name was not literally Jezebel. The Lord names people based on their character. The Lord called her Jezebel because she did what the infamous Jezebel did as recorded in the Hebrew Bible. (See First Kings 16:31-21:25; Second Kings 9:30-37.) She is considered to be the most evil woman who ever lived. Even in our modern world, names are still powerful. For example, who names their daughter Jezebel? So what was so terrible about Jezebel that her name would be associated with evil throughout history?

A little background is necessary to understand the seriousness of God's concern. Before God allowed the Hebrews to enter the Land of Promise, He gave them a stern warning not to intermarry with the pagans, nor participate in any of their worship.

We read in Exodus:

> *Observe what I command you this day. Behold I am driving out from before you the Amorite and the Canaanite and the Hittite and the Perizzite and the Hivite and the Jebusite. Take heed to yourselves, lest you make a covenant with the inhabitants of the land where you are going, lest it be a snare in your midst.*

> *But you shall destroy their altars, break their sacred pillars, and cut down their wooden images (for you shall worship no other god, for the LORD, whose name is Jealous, is a jealous God), lest you make a covenant with the inhabitants of the land, and they play the harlot with their gods and make sacrifice to their gods, and one of them invites you and you eat of his sacrifice, and you take of his daughters for your sons, and his daughters play the harlot with their gods and make your sons play the harlot with their gods* (Exodus 34:11-16).

We see that God considers idolatry and immorality as spiritual adultery and unfaithfulness to Him. Like a husband is jealous for his wife to be faithful to her marriage vows, how much more the Lord desires the same of His people. Yet, for political and economic reasons, King Ahab married a daughter of the king of Sidon. The Sidonians worshiped and served Ba'al (meaning lord). Ba'al was a rival to the One True God of Abraham, Isaac, and Jacob. As it was with all pagan deities, Ba'al worship was accompanied by sacrifices and immoral behavior.

When Ahab married Jezebel, she persuaded Ahab to join her in Ba'al worship and to impose Ba'al worship on the people in the northern kingdom of Israel. They were so successful, the people were forsaking the One True God for Ba'al. Jezebel was very persuasive and seductive. It all seemed innocent to the naïve and undiscerning. Just add a little Ba'al worship along with your worship of YHVH. But it wasn't long before the people preferred the carnal, sensual worship of Ba'al.

To please Jezebel, Ahab built a temple and altar to Ba'al in Samaria. She invited the 450 prophets of Ba'al, plus the 400 prophets of Asherah (Ba'al's female consort) to feast with her at her table. To make matters worse, Jezebel killed as many of God's prophets as she could find. Worship of Ba'al was spreading so fast that it was threatening to supplant worship of the God of Israel.

Finally, there was a showdown between the God of Israel and Ba'al when Elijah challenged the prophets of Ba'al on Mt. Carmel. When the God of Israel showed Himself as the One True God, Elijah had all of Ba'al's prophets executed. When this news reached Jezebel, she put out a "hit" on Elijah, who fled for his life.

God promised to destroy Ahab's family as judgment for his allowing his wife to kill God's prophets. It was Jezebel who had Naboth murdered in order to take his vineyard for Ahab. When Elijah heard about this heinous act, he prophesied to Ahab that God would judge him as a result, and that dogs would eat Jezebel's body at the wall of Jezreel. This prophecy was fulfilled 11 years after the death of Ahab. The only thing the dogs left was Jezebel's skull, feet, and the palms of her hands.

When we read the story of Ahab and Jezebel, we realize that Ahab was a weak-willed man, leader, and king. Jezebel was the much stronger personality and the real power behind the throne. Ahab was not able or willing to exercise his authority over Jezebel. We read in First Kings 21:25, *"But there was no one like Ahab who sold himself to do wickedness in the sight of the Lord, because Jezebel his wife stirred him up."*

In spite of his evil ways, when Elijah confronted Ahab, he humbled himself and repented. As a result, God had mercy on Ahab and delayed His judgment on Ahab to his children's generation.

Now back to Thyatira. The Jezebel of Thyatira was having a similar influence on the congregation as the real Jezebel was on the children of Israel. The Jezebel of Thyatira was a self-proclaimed prophetess. She presented herself as an oracle of God. But she was really an oracle for satan.

She was teaching the believers that it was OK for them to participate in the idolatry and immorality that was part of the trade guild ceremonies. If they participated, the Lord considered their involvement to be spiritual adultery. If they refused to participate, they might lose their jobs and would certainly be shunned socially.

What is the believer to do? To solve their dilemma, the false prophetess claimed to have a "word from God." She said that they could have the best of both worlds. They could worship the God of Abraham, Isaac, and Jacob while at the same time taking part in the religious ceremonies of their guild. Perhaps her persuasive reasoning was that God's grace would allow for such a compromise. Also, since the believers knew that Apollo was not really a god, there was no harm in participating. Furthermore, how else would they "witness" to their lost friends in the guild?

What to the Lord was a clear black and white issue, the false prophetess made a grey issue that appealed to the material and economic needs of the people. Some in the congregation were persuaded by her "prophetic anointing," and it was leading them astray.

As I have mentioned, eating meat offered to idols was not the issue. This meat was readily available in the marketplace and at discounted prices. Paul said in Romans 14 and First Corinthians 8 and 10 that purchasing meat in the marketplace that had been offered to idols was an individual matter of choice.

But participating in eating meat offered to idols at a religious ceremony was a different issue. That was a form of worship that showed communion and fellowship with the deity. It often led to debauchery and sexual immorality as part of the worship. This is what James instructed the new Gentile converts to avoid. Acts 15:20 reads, *"but that we write to them to abstain from things polluted by idols, from sexual immorality, from things strangled, and from blood."* Paul also strongly spoke against this in First Corinthians 10:14-22.

The Son of Man is gracious and merciful toward His people. He always gives us time to repent and judge ourselves. But if we fail to do so, He will judge us. For believers, His judgment and chastening is corrective for our own good and has redeeming value for us. For unbelievers, His judgment is separation from Him.

At Thyatira, the Lord had given the false prophetess time to repent, but she refused, and the leadership of the congregation refused to judge her words. Like Ahab, they were too weak to use their spiritual authority to cast her out of the congregation. They did not test nor challenge the "prophetic word." Neither did the congregants who were following her. Like the city itself, the congregation was in danger of becoming a citadel or stronghold of idolatry and immorality. Yet, even now, if they humble themselves and repent, the Lord is ready to forgive.

However if the false prophetess and those who are following her do not repent, He will judge them Himself. His strongly worded warning is very graphic. The Lord will remove His hedge of protection and mercy and give them over to their own sins. Sin carries within it its own seeds of destruction. God will give them up to their own lusts, which will destroy them.

Paul gave this warning to the believers in Galatia:

> Do not be deceived, God is not mocked; for whatever a man sows, that he will also reap. For he who sows to his flesh will of the flesh reap corruption, but he who sows to the Spirit will of the Spirit reap everlasting life (Galatians 6:7-8).

Because the false prophetess sowed spiritual and physical adultery, she and her followers will reap the judgment of such sins in their own bodies. The Lord says He will *"cast her into a sick bed"* (Rev. 2:22), which is a Jewish idiom that means she will be afflicted with illness caused by her own immorality. When God's people see His judgment on her and her followers, they will see firsthand that He who has eyes of fire searches their minds and hearts and rewards them according to their righteous deeds.

Whereas the false prophetess claimed to be speaking for God, the Son of Man says she is teaching the doctrines of satan. He then reminds those who have not followed this woman to hold on to what they know to be true from God's Holy Word. While God has His true prophets, their words will always be in agreement with the Scriptures. The leaders at Thyatira should stop seeking a "prophetic word" from someone who claims to speak for God, and just obey what God has already told them to do in His Word.

Is there a message for us in this 2,000-year-old letter? Is there something for us to learn? The answer is a clear *yes!* There are four very important insights we can gain from this prophetic message that are particularly critical for our times.

1. Beware of False Prophets

Jesus warned us against false prophets:

> *Beware of false prophets, who come to you in sheep's cloth-ing, but inwardly they are ravenous wolves. You will know them by their fruits…Not everyone who says to Me, "Lord, Lord," shall enter the kingdom of heaven, but he who does the will of My Father in heaven.*

> *Many will say to Me in that day, "Lord, Lord, have we not prophesied in Your name, cast out demons in Your name, and done many wonders in Your name?" And then I will declare to them, "I never knew you; depart from Me, you who practice lawlessness!"* (Matthew 7:15-16;21-23).

This is a strong warning that miraculous signs and wonders are not the true test of a prophet from the Lord.

There have always been false prophets and prophetesses in the universal body of believers as well as in local congregations. Their numbers will increase as we get closer to the end of days. Jesus said this Himself in His teaching about the endtimes: *"Then many false prophets will rise up and deceive many"* (Matt. 24:11).

Peter warned of false prophets and false teachers:

> *But there were also false prophets among the people, even as there will be false teachers among you, who will secretly bring in destructive heresies, even denying the Lord who bought them, and bring on themselves swift destruction. And many will follow their destructive ways, because of whom the way of truth will be blasphemed. By covetous-ness they will exploit you with deceptive words; for a long*

time their judgment has not been idle, and their destruc-
tion does not slumber (2 Peter 2:1-3).

In the Book of Revelation, John tells us about the Beast from the Earth who is the False Prophet. John writes:

> *He performs great signs, so that he even makes fire come down from heaven on the earth in the sight of men. And he deceives those who dwell on the earth by those signs which he was granted to do in the sight of the beast, tell-ing those who dwell on the earth to make an image of the beast who was wounded by the sword and lived* (Revela-tion 13:13-14).

We can tell true prophets of God from false prophets by examining their life and their words. True prophets of God will bear the fruit of the Spirit; will walk in holiness, obeying the Lord; will have a wholesome fear of the Lord; and will focus their ministry and words on the charac-ter of God and the centrality of Jesus as Lord. Furthermore, their words will always be in accordance with the Scriptures.

True prophets will be anointed of God, and that anointing will be obvious. While God gives His true prophets a measure of charisma, we must not follow charisma which can be counterfeited. We must inspect the spiritual fruit and follow only those who express the character of God in their lives.

God certainly has His true prophets, and they are much needed. A prophetic word that is truly from God spoken to our spirit can be most refreshing, encouraging, and comforting. We all need that from time to time. But we don't need to be running from meeting to meeting "seek-ing the prophetic" in place of spending time alone with God to hear Him for ourselves. Let the people say, "Amen!"

2. God Holds Leaders Responsible for Guarding His People

The primary reason why the false prophetess was able to continue her disastrous teaching in the congregation at Thyatira was because the leadership was weak. When God calls people to a leadership role, He gives them an anointing and spiritual authority that equips them to serve. The leaders at Thyatira did not exercise their God-given authority to rebuke and correct the woman, and if necessary, cast her out of the congregation.

Leaders have three primary responsibilities to the people they serve. These are: 1) shepherding, 2) teaching, and 3) guarding (protecting). The Scripture is clear that God's leaders are not to rule over the people, but to serve them and be an example for the people to emulate.

Peter writes to the elders:

> *Shepherd the flock of God which is among you, serving as overseers, not by compulsion but willingly, not for dishonest gain but eagerly; nor as being lords over those entrusted to you, but being examples to the flock* (1 Peter 5:2-3).

Paul exhorted the elders at Ephesus:

> *Therefore take heed to yourselves and to all the flock, among which the Holy Spirit has made you overseers, to shepherd [guard] the church [congregation] of God which He purchased with His own blood. For I know this, that after my departure savage wolves will come in among you, not sparing the flock. Also from among yourselves men will rise up, speaking perverse things, to draw away the disciples after themselves* (Acts 20:28-30).

Paul wrote to Timothy:

Let no one despise your youth, but be an example to the believers in word, in conduct, in love, in spirit, in faith, in purity. Till I come, give attention to reading, to exhortation, to doctrine. Do not neglect the gift that is in you, which was given to you by prophecy with the laying on of hands of the eldership (1 Timothy 4:12-14).

Paul wrote a second letter to Timothy and instructed him with these words:

Preach the word! Be ready in season and out of season. Convince, rebuke, exhort, with all longsuffering and teaching. For the time will come when they will not endure sound doctrine, but according to their own desires, because they have itching ears, they will heap up for themselves teachers; and they will turn their ears away from the truth, and be turned aside to fables. But you be watchful in all things, endure afflictions, do the work of an evangelist, fulfill your ministry (2 Timothy 4:2-5).

Paul further instructed Timothy:

And a servant of the Lord must not quarrel but be gentle to all, able to teach, patient, in humility correcting those who are in opposition, if God perhaps will grant them repentance so that they may know the truth, and that they may come to their senses and escape the snare of the devil, having been taken captive by him to do his will (2 Timothy 2:24-26).

3. Believers Have a Responsibility to Test the Spirits

Just because someone says, "Thus saith the Lord" does not mean that the Lord is speaking through the person. It may be the devil speaking through the person or it may be their own soul speaking. In 36 years of ministry, the Lord has spoken to me numerous times, and He never used King James English.

Paul wrote to the believers at Thessalonica, *"Do not quench the Spirit. Do not despise prophecies"* (1 Thess. 5:19-20). We should embrace the gifts of the Spirit, including prophetic words. This is important for a healthy spiritual life. On the other hand, we must not be naïve and believe that everything we are told is from God really *is* from God. So Paul says in the next verse, *"Test all things; hold fast what is good"* (1 Thess. 5:21).

John wrote, *"Beloved, do not believe every spirit, but test the spirits, whether they are of God; because many false prophets have gone out into the world"* (1 John 4:1).

Just because someone has a lot of charisma and a television program does not mean he is a true prophet of God or that he has a genuine charismatic gift of prophecy. We should have people in our midst who judge prophecies to see if they are truly from God (see 1 Cor. 14:29). This is not an option.

This is what the people did at Berea. Acts 17:10-11 informs us:

> *Then the brethren immediately sent Paul and Silas away by night to Berea. When they arrived, they went into the synagogue of the Jews. These were more fair-minded than those in Thessalonica, in that they received the word with all readiness, and searched the Scriptures daily to find out whether these things were so.*

4. Believers Must Live Holy Lives

Because of centuries of Judeo-Christianity, we no longer have to make sacrifices to an idol nor participate in orgies to be successful, have a job, and be accepted in our communities. But the same temptations are just as real today; they have just changed forms.

Tragically, our culture has broken up its Judeo-Christian moral foundations. The pursuits of the lust of the flesh, the lust of the eyes, and the pride of life have replaced the pursuit of God. These are our new gods. As a result, our society has lost its fear of God. When people lose their fear of God, there are few restraints on the way they behave. Our culture and society now permits any form of godless behavior, and there is no shame to our sins.

Sadly, the values, attitudes, lifestyle, and morals of many professing believers are not much different than that of unbelievers. While believers do not worship an image of a god or goddess, whatever we put as the goal of our lives before God becomes an idol. Whatever we spend our time and money and energy to achieve in place of knowing and serving God becomes an idol. It may be the god of pleasure, power, money, ambition, getting ahead, climbing to the top, pride, ego, or even family and friends. We are all challenged to overcome these temptations in our everyday lives.

More and more we read about corrupt and unfaithful "Christian" politicians. Professing Christian business people are overcome by greed. Professing Christian women often dress as immodestly as unbelievers. Professing Christian sports stars take steroids to give themselves an unfair advantage in competition. Professing Christian entertainers struggle with many of the same vices as the secular counterparts. Christian men and woman struggle with staying pure. Christian families are torn apart by debt. In every area of our lives, believers are confronted with the temptation of compromise.

We don't need to go to a prophetic conference to "get a word from the Lord." He has already told us what He wants us to hear. If we will spend quality time in God's Word and listen to His voice, we might hear Him say something like the following:

You are the salt of the earth; but if salt loses its flavor, how shall it be seasoned? It is then good for nothing but to be thrown out and trampled under foot by men. You are the light of the world. A city that is set on a hill cannot be hidden. Nor do they light a lamp and put it under a basket, but on a lampstand, and it gives light to all who are in the house. Let your light so shine before men, that they may see your good works and glorify your Father in heaven (Matthew 5:13-16).

The Promise (verses 26-28)

To those who overcome the temptation at Thyatira and remain faithful, the Lord makes them a wonderful promise. He says they will rule with Him over the nations. Jesus refers to the promise His Father made to Him in Psalm 2:

> *I will declare the decree: The LORD has said to Me, "You are My Son, today I have begotten You. Ask of Me, and I will give You the nations for Your inheritance, and the ends of the earth for Your possession. You shall break them with a rod of iron; You shall dash them to pieces like a potter's vessel"* (Psalms 2:7-9).

Furthermore, Jesus promises to give them the morning star. Literally, the morning star is actually not a star but the planet Venus, which is the brightest object in the sky after the sun and moon. It is the "star" that appears just before sunrise and signals the end of night and the beginning of a new day. Because of its brightness and time of appearing, ancient people worshiped Venus as a goddess. If you don't want to get up early to view the morning star, you can see it on the Internet and still sleep late.

The name morning star was also given to lucifer since he was the most beautiful angel in Heaven (see Isa. 14:12). But when he sinned, his name was changed to satan, the adversary of God and God's people. The appearance of the morning star every day just before sunlight is a message from Heaven that God judged lucifer because of his pride by casting him away from His presence.

Because He radiates the glory of God, Jesus is the true morning star who leads us out of darkness into the new day of His marvelous light. His countenance is *"like the sun shining in its strength"* (Rev. 1:16). In Revelation 22:16, Jesus calls Himself *"the Bright and Morning Star."*

Peter adds, *"And so we have the prophetic word confirmed, which you do well to heed as a light that shines in a dark place, until the day dawns and the morning star rises in your hearts"* (2 Peter 1:19).

The Lord ends His message as He does all the others, by exhorting the receivers of His message to hear what God's Spirit is saying to them. Those who hear and overcome will rule and reign with the Son of Man and live with Him in His glory for eternity.

If the Lord's message to Thyatira applies to your organization, your ministry, or your life, let us repent and do what He says so we can be overcomers. Let us heed the words of Paul who wrote, *"Test* [prove] *all things; hold fast what is good. Abstain from every form of evil"* (1 Thess. 5:21-22).

He who has an ear, let him hear.

REVIEW QUESTIONS

1. Write a summary of what you have learned in this lesson. Write the summary in clear concise words as if you are going to present it to another person.

2. Write an explanation of how you can apply what you have learned in this lesson to your life.

3. Share what you have learned with your family, friends, and members of your study group.

Chapter 10

The Letter to Sardis

REVELATION REVIEW

WHEN we learn the circumstances the believers were experiencing in these seven congregations, it is only by the mercy of God that any of them survived. Thyatira was no exception. Living in a trade guild union town, the believers were constantly faced with the issue of idol worship. Since each trade guild was devoted to a particular god or goddess, the members of that union were expected to participate in the sacrifices made to their deity. The pagans did not give this a second thought. This was not an issue to them. But for the believers, it was an issue.

Put yourself in the shoes (sandals) of a believer when he or she arrives at the union hall. The leader calls the meeting to order, at which time prayers and sacrifices are made to the patron deity. Then, to show union with the deity, you are required to eat the remainder of the sacrifice. When appropriate, this "worship service" is accompanied by unholy revelry, the likes of which depends on the nature of the deity. Do you think you could do this? If you don't, it could cost you your job or even your life. Perhaps you have a wife and kids. You have a family to feed, bills to pay, etc. What are you going to do?

The Lord saw their situation and sent the congregation at Thyatira a letter of encouragement. In spite of their challenges, He praised them for their works, their love, their service, their faith, their patience, and their spiritual progress. Now, I don't know about you, but I would be thrilled if the Lord spoke these words to me.

However, there was a woman in the congregation who was telling the people that it was OK for them to participate in the pagan worship services. The Lord called her Jezebel after the infamous Jezebel in the Hebrew Bible. This woman claimed to speak for God. We modern believers should know better than to fall for this lying deception.

But how about the believers at Thyatira? Christianity was a new faith and they were new believers. The supposed prophetic word from God could all be very confusing, particularly when it was what they wanted to hear. Even today, I marvel at what some Christians will accept and believe to be God's prophetic word speaking to them. While the Lord gave some wonderful promises to the overcomers, He only had harsh words to those who did not repent.

The Lord's message to the believers at Thyatira is so relevant to us today. As our world becomes more and more anti-God, we too will have to make hard choices. We too will be faced with situations that we never dreamed would happen and decisions that we have never before had to make. As this conflict and tension increases, many Jezebels will arise who claim to speak for God. May we test the spirits and have the spiritual wisdom, strength, and courage to live holy lives.

After sending His letter to the believes at Thyatira, the Lord has a Word for the congregation at Sardis. Before reading His letter, let's learn about the city so we can understand why the Lord wrote this letter to this group of believers who at one time were full of spiritual life but are now spiritually dead.

BACKGROUND

After John's letter was read to the congregation at Thyatira, God's special courier traveled about 35 miles southeast to Sardis. In its early history, Sardis had been a very powerful and prosperous city. It was the capital of the ancient kingdom of Lydia and was famous for its wealth.

The prominent feature of Sardis was its elevation. The citadel of Sardis was built on top of a 400-foot-high hill that was protected by steep cliffs thought impossible to climb. Because of its location, the citizens of Sardis considered the city to be an impenetrable fortress. When the city was attacked, the citizens living in the valley below would flee to the citadel for refuge. A good example like Sardis we can relate to is Masada in Israel.

Since the citizens of Sardis felt so secure from enemy attack, they failed to provide watchmen to guard the city. They went to sleep happily, thinking they were safe and secure. But it was a false sense of security. The citadel was attacked at night on two different occasions. In 547 B.C., the Persian King Cyrus made a surprise attack and captured the city.

Sardis then became the seat of the Persian governor for the region. Later, when Alexander approached the city, the Persian leaders came out of the citadel and surrendered to him without a fight. Then, around 214 B.C., Antiochus the Great captured the city in another surprise night attack. Antiochus eventually abandoned Sardis, at which time it came under the rule of the Pergamos kingdom, and finally, under the rule of Rome.

Sardis was destroyed by a catastrophic earthquake in A.D. 17. Since Sardis was a Roman province, the Roman Emperor Tiberius made a generous donation to help rebuild the city. As a show of gratitude, Sardis petitioned Rome to build a temple for imperial cult worship, but the petition was denied. Historians explain that the Sardis appeal was based on their past glory and greatness rather than on an expectation of future prosperity.

The name Sardis means *renewal.* It had a name and reputation of greatness in the past, but was now struggling to renew itself. With help from Tiberius, Sardis had recovered to a degree, but was no longer prominent as it had been in the past. Compared to its former glory, Sardis was in a gradual state of decline, and in some ways was a dead city.

At the bottom of the citadel in the lower city, there was a theater, a stadium, and a huge temple to the goddess Artemis. Artemis was the Greek name of Diana, the goddess of fertility. Archaeologists and historians tell us that the temple to Artemis was so great that it had never actually been completely finished. It was the largest Greek temple in the ancient world. Some of the columns of the temple are still standing today. As with all idolatry, the worship of Artemis was accompanied by gross immorality and every imaginable form of depravity.

Sardis was well known for its textile industry, and its people claimed to have discovered the art of dyeing wool. It was a major manufacturing center of everyday garments worn by common people, plus a white garment worn by both priests and ordinary people at religious ceremonies and in victory parades. This would include the many priests who served at the temple to Artemis.

There was a large Jewish community at Sardis. Archaeologists have uncovered the synagogue, which was one of the largest in the ancient world. Apparently, Sardis was one of the few cities where the Jews and early believers coexisted peaceably.

Today, Sardis lies entirely in ruins, and is an archaeological site near the small village named Sart. The main ruins are of the synagogue, the temple to Artemis, and a Byzantine church building. With this brief background, let's read the prophetic message from the Son of Man to the congregation at Sardis.

To the Congregation at Sardis (Revelation 3:1-6) The Greeting (verse 1)

In His greeting to the Sardis congregation, the Lord identifies Himself as the One *"who has the seven Spirits of God and the seven stars."* In the Bible, the number seven, when connected to God, means perfection. So when Jesus says He *"has the seven Spirits of God,"* He is referring to the Holy Spirit, or as noted earlier, in Hebrew, *Ruach HaKodesh*. We find the same phrase in Revelation 1:4 and 5:6.

Isaiah speaks of the sevenfold character of the Holy Spirit and the Messiah:

> *There shall come forth a Rod from the stem of Jesse, and a Branch shall grow out of his roots. The Spirit of the Lord shall rest upon Him, the Spirit of wisdom and understanding, the Spirit of counsel and might, the Spirit of knowledge and of the fear of the Lord* (Isaiah 11:1-2).

The Hebrew word translated as "branch" is *netzer*, which means resident (*natzrati*) of Nazareth (*Natzeret*). Isaiah is predicting that the sevenfold Spirit of God will rest upon the Nazarene.

Matthew refers to the Isaiah passage and says, *"And he came and dwelt in a city called Nazareth, that it might be fulfilled which was spoken by the prophets, 'He shall be called a Nazarene'"* (Matt. 2:23). In Israel today, Christians are called *Notzrim*, which means followers of the man from *Natzeret*.

When Jesus was baptized, the Spirit of God rested or descended upon Him, as we learn in Matthew 3:

> *When He had been baptized, Jesus came up immediately from the water; and behold, the heavens were opened to Him, and He saw the Spirit of God descending like a dove and alighting upon Him. And suddenly a voice came from*

heaven, saying, "This is My beloved Son, in whom I am well pleased [presenting, announcing, bringing forth]" (Matthew 3:16-17).

When Jesus began His ministry in Nazareth, He went to the synagogue and read Isaiah 61:1-2, which was the text for that particular Sabbath reading. Luke records it for us:

So He came to Nazareth, where He had been brought up. And as His custom was, He went into the synagogue on the Sabbath day, and stood up to read. And He was handed the book of the prophet Isaiah. And when He opened the book, He found the place where it was written; "The Spirit of the LORD is upon Me, because He has anointed Me to preach the Gospel to the poor; He has sent Me to heal the broken hearted; to proclaim liberty to the captives and recovery of sight to the blind, to set at liberty those who are oppressed; to proclaim the acceptable year of the LORD."

Then He closed the book, and gave it back to the attendant and sat down. And the eyes of all who were in the synagogue were fixed on Him. And He began to say to them, "Today this Scripture is fulfilled in your hearing" (Luke 4:16-21).

In Isaiah 42, God says He will put His Spirit on His Chosen One and the Gentiles will come to Him. Matthew refers to Isaiah 42 and says of Jesus:

Behold! My Servant whom I have chosen, My Beloved in whom My soul is well pleased! I will put My Spirit upon Him, and He will declare justice to the Gentiles. He will not quarrel nor cry out, nor will anyone hear His voice in the streets. A bruised reed He will not break, and smoking flax He will not quench, till He sends forth justice to victory; and in His name Gentiles will trust (Matthew 12:18-21).

Jesus not only tells the congregation that He has the Holy Spirit, He also says that He has the seven stars, which we learned in Revelation 1:20 represent the leaders of the seven congregations. In other words, Jesus is Lord over His people and the leaders are accountable to Him. Now why would the Lord greet them in this way? As we will discover in the rest of this chapter, they are spiritually dead and in great need of a spiritual renewal and awakening.

The Rebuke (verses 2-3)

Regrettably, the Lord had nothing praiseworthy to say to the leaders or the congregation of Sardis as a whole. When He says He knows their works, He is informing them that He is fully and completely aware of their spiritual condition. While they have a reputation as being an "alive congregation," except for a few, they are spiritually dead.

The congregation was a mirror image of the city. Sardis boasted of its past glory and greatness. It had a name or reputation throughout the region for its fortress location, its wealth, its textile industry, and its great temple to Artemis. While the city worked hard to recover from the earthquake, it would never regain its place of prominence. The once great, proud city was in decline.

Likewise, the community of believers at Sardis gloried in its past. We don't know who first brought the Gospel to Sardis or when the congregation was birthed. But like the city, the congregation must have had an exciting spiritual history. It was still known throughout the region for its spiritual reputation. But that was all in the past.

Now they were spiritually dead and in great need of renewal and revival. This is why Jesus greeted them as the One who has the Holy

Spirit. They need a fresh outpouring of the Holy Spirit to renew their spiritual strength and vitality. Like the temple to Artemis that was never completed, the local congregation of believers had not completed the work the Lord wanted to accomplish at Sardis.

There are entire denominations and many local congregations today that are just like the believers at Sardis. They have had wonderful spiritual experiences with God in the past, but not much lately. They talk about how God worked powerfully through the founders of their denomination or congregation. That was all in the past. While they glory in the past, they do not have a *current* testimony of the Lord working in their midst. Maintaining their traditions has become more important to them than a fresh move of God. They are more concerned with form than they are with spiritual life. They love their system more than they love the Lord. They have replaced a dynamic relationship with the Lord with their programs.

They may have beautiful buildings and even stained glass windows, but they have no life. They have a name or reputation in the city, but they are spiritually dead. They need a fresh outpouring of the Spirit of the Living God. The Lord tells them five things they must do or else they will not survive.

1. Be Watchful

First, He tells them to be watchful or alert. In Bible times, one of the most critical positions in a city was that of the watchman. The watchman had only one responsibility, which was to stay at his post on the city wall and watch for any approaching enemy. The whole city depended on the watchman. He had to be awake and sober. As soon as the watchman saw the enemy approaching, he would sound an alarm so the people could prepare to defend themselves.

We can clearly see how the role of the watchman was so critical at Sardis. Because of their strategic location, Sardis thought it was safe from any attack. As a result, the city did not post a watchman to guard the city. Due to this false confidence, Sardis was defeated on two different occasions by a surprise night attack.

The community of believers had made the same mistake. They had not been watching for their spiritual enemies who were always looking for an opportunity to attack them. The congregation was not alert. They were complacent, thinking that their glorious past was enough to protect them from spiritual decline. The Lord is warning them that they will not survive unless they wake up spiritually.

This Word is certainly relevant today as the historic protestant denominations, many local congregations, and individual believers have gone to sleep spiritually. They need to wake up. They have not fulfilled their high calling and destiny as a witness to the love and power of God.

Paul wrote to the believers at Ephesus, *"Awake, you who sleep, arise from the dead, and Christ* [Messiah] *will give you light"* (Eph. 5:14).

2. Strengthen

The second thing the Lord tells them to do is to strengthen the things which remain, as the little spiritual life they have is about to die. When Sardis realized it was under attack, the citizens did the best they could to defend themselves. They desperately tried to repair the breaches in the walls and reinforce or strengthen what had not yet fallen (that which remained). But it was too little, too late. Sardis fell and the defenders of the city died.

The Lord uses the history of Sardis as a warning to the congregation. If they don't wake up and seek God for a fresh outpouring of His Spirit, the little spiritual life they have left will also die. Any discerning spiritual leader as well as ordinary believers should realize this Word is clearly relevant for us today. Because they have forsaken God's Word and compromised their convictions, the historic Christian denominations are dying physically and spiritually before our eyes. If they don't strengthen the little spiritual life they have left, they will be completely dead.

The same is true for many local assemblies of believers as well as individuals who profess Christianity. Let us humbly examine ourselves to see how this word from the Lord might apply to our own Christian life and experience. Are we dead or alive? Do we glory only in what God did in the past, or do we have a fresh testimony of God's Spirit working in our lives?

3. Remember

The third word the Lord gave to the congregation at Sardis was to remember. He calls them to remember how they had received and heard. What had they received and heard? They had received and heard the Word of God. It is God's holy Word ministered in the power of the Holy Spirit that changes lives.

Paul explained to Timothy:

> But you must continue in the things which you have learned and been assured of, knowing from whom you have learned them, and that from childhood you have known the Holy Scriptures, which are able to make you wise for salvation through faith which is in Christ [Messiah] Jesus. All Scripture is given by inspiration from God, and is profitable for doctrine, for reproof, for correction, for instruction in righteousness, that that the man of God may be complete, thoroughly equipped for every good work (2 Timothy 3:14-17).

In this passage, Paul explains the Scriptures are "God-breathed," meaning that God spoke His words out of His own mouth. Whatever God speaks has God's own life in His words. Therefore, God's spoken Words have the power to change people's lives.

Paul further exhorted Timothy:

> *Preach the word! Be ready in season and out of season. Convince, rebuke, exhort, with all longsuffering and teaching. For the time will come when they will not endure sound doctrine, but according to their own desires, because they have itching ears, they will heap up on themselves teachers; and they will turn their ears away from the truth, and be turned aside to fables. But you be watchful in all things, endure afflictions, do the work of an evangelist, fulfill your ministry* (2 Timothy 4:2-5).

The community of believers at Sardis was no longer preaching and teaching God's holy Word. As a result, the people were not being grounded in their faith; they were not being convicted about their sins; they were not being corrected and challenged; they were not being taught. They were losing their witness to the city. The solution to this condition was to get back to the basics of proclaiming the Word of God.

Is this warning from the Lord relevant to us today? Unfortunately, the answer is *yes!* Once again, we see that much of Western and American Christianity no longer believes nor proclaims God's Word. Under the banner of the "Higher Criticism" of Scriptures, seminaries teach their future ministers that the Bible is not really the Word of God, that the miracles of Jesus are "fairy tales," and that the Bible is an antiquated book written by men that is not relevant to our modern world.

When the seminary students graduate and are given a congregation, they pass on what they have learned to their congregants. The result is that church buildings all across America are filled with decent people who don't hear the Word of God, don't know the Word of God, and don't believe the Word of God.

The denominational leaders need to remember that it was the Word of God that was working mightily through their founders. They need to return to proclaiming God's holy Word. If they don't heed this warning, what little spiritual life they have left will die. If these words pierce your heart, then do what the Lord says. Let God use you to bring spiritual renewal to your denomination and local congregation. Do it now while there is still a little life left.

4. Hold Fast

The fourth instruction the Lord gave to the believers at Sardis was to hold fast. To hold fast to something means to cling to it with all your might and not let go. Some Bible versions translate the phrase *hold fast* as *obey it*.

What does the Lord want them to hold fast and obey? In the context of His letter, He wants them to hold fast and obey what He has told them. He wants them to be watchful of their spiritual condition, to strengthen the spiritual life that remains, and to remember to proclaim His Word.

Sardis did its best to hold on to its past, but it failed. The city was in a state of perpetual decline. It never regained its prominence. As mentioned earlier, when Sardis petitioned Rome to establish the temple for emperor worship, Rome rejected the petition. The Lord warns the congregation at Sardis that they will end up just like the city unless they hold fast and obey His prophetic word to them.

Paul gave a similar exhortation to Timothy:

> *Hold fast the pattern of sound words which you have heard from me, in faith and love which are in Christ* [Messiah] *Jesus. That good thing which was committed to you, keep by the Holy Spirit who dwells in us* (2 Timothy 1:13-14).

Once again we ask the question, "Are the Lord's words relevant to the Christian world of today?" Do Christian leaders today need to be watchful of their spiritual condition? Do they need to strengthen the little spiritual life that remains? Do they need to remember to proclaim the Word of God? Absolutely, the answer is *yes!* If they want to regain their spiritual life, they must do these things. They must do them now! This leads us to the fifth statement that the Lord made to the believers at Sardis.

5. Repent

Jesus told them to repent. The believers at Sardis had a religious spirit, but they did not have the Holy Spirit working in their midst. They had dead works, not spiritual ministry. They preached sermons, but did not proclaim the Word of God. They had form without function, and rituals without revival. They had creeds without deeds, services without serving, and meetings without ministry.

They must awaken to their spiritual condition, strengthen the little that remains, proclaim God's Word, hold fast, and obey the Lord's warnings, and repent. If they do not do these things, the Lord will come when they least expect it, to judge them. They will be as unprepared and surprised as the city of Sardis was when it was overthrown by surprise attack at night. The Lord Himself will withdraw His presence, His protection, and His provision, and they will not survive as a believing community.

The Lord is certainly calling Western Christianity to repent of the same issues He raised with the believers at Sardis. If we do not respond to His grace and mercy, we will see His holy justice. Many believe this is already happening. You can be a part of the solution and not the problem by acting on the Lord's Words.

The Promise (verses 4-6)

Although the Lord has nothing praiseworthy to say to the leaders or the congregation as a whole, He does say that there are a few believers who have remained faithful. Throughout history, no matter how much organized Christianity has failed, God has always had a remnant that stayed true to the faith and lived godly lives. They often were persecuted, and many were martyred, but they persevered.

The Lord made the following promise to this faithful remnant. First He acknowledges their faithfulness by saying they have not defiled or soiled their garments. Ordinary people of the Greco-Roman world wore white garments at religious ceremonies and in victory parades. When the Roman general returned to Rome after defeating the enemy, Rome had a great victory parade called "The Parade of Triumph." All the citizens of Rome turned out for the parade, and they all wore clean, white garments.

As mentioned previously, there were many priests who wore white garments while serving at the great temple of Artemis. They certainly would not wear a soiled garment, as that would be a sign of defilement. They would not be worthy to serve at the temple.

We have an example of this in Zechariah, with Joshua the high priest standing before the Angel of the Lord in soiled garments. Zechariah writes:

> Then he showed me Joshua the high priest standing before the Angel of the LORD, and satan standing at his right hand to oppose him. And the LORD said to satan, "The LORD rebuke you, satan! The LORD who has chosen Jerusalem rebuke you! Is this not a brand plucked from the fire?" Now Joshua was clothed with filthy garments, and was standing before the Angel. Then He answered and spoke to those who stood before Him, saying, "Take away the filthy garments from him." And to him He said, "See, I have removed your iniquity from you, and I will cloth you with rich robes." And I said, "Let them put a clean turban on his head." So they put a clean turban on his head, and they put the clothes on him. And the Angel of the LORD stood by (Zechariah 3:1-5).

With this background information of both the secular and spiritual connotation of clean, white garments, we can better understand and appreciate the first promise the Lord give to the faithful remnant. He says that they will walk with Him in white garments. The white garments symbolized moral and spiritual purity and victory over the enemy. The Lord made this promise to the faithful because they were living pure lives and were victorious over the spiritual challenges they faced. The Lord says they are worthy. In other words, they have clean garments.

There is a worthiness that is imputed to us by the righteousness of Jesus which is credited to us when we put our faith and trust in Him as our perfect representative before God. But there is also an imparted righteousness which is based on our walk with God. Jesus says that the remnant are worthy because they have not soiled their garments.

What this means is that while our eternal destiny in Heaven is based on the righteousness of Jesus, our actual place and glory in Heaven is based on our acting on the divinely imparted righteousness to live holy lives and walk in victory over sin. While all true believers will be in the great Parade of Triumph in Heaven, those who have lived godly lives and have overcome in spiritual conflict will be, we might say, at the head of the parade. The Book of Revelation mentions white garments six additional times. (See Revelation 3:18; 4:4; 6:11; 7:9,13; 19:14.)

The second promise the Lord makes to the faithful at Sardis is that He will not erase their names from the Book of Life. In ancient times, cities had a registry book that listed the names of all the citizens. When they died, or if they had committed a crime, their names would be erased from the book of citizens.

There is a Scripture in Isaiah that tells us that the citizens in Jerusalem have their names in the city registry. Isaiah 4:3 reads, *"And it shall come to pass that he who is left in Zion and remains in Jerusalem will be called holy—everyone who is recorded among the living in Jerusalem."*

We have similar registry books today. For example, we have to register for social security, to get our driver's license or voter ID, to join an organization, to be put on a mailing list, or to be placed on the roll of a local congregation. If we die or commit a crime, our names are removed or, using Bible language, blotted out from the registry.

Likewise, the Bible says that God has a registry of all the citizens of Heaven. It is called the Book of Life. We first hear about this "heavenly registry" in the Book of Exodus when Moses pleaded with God not to blot out the children of Israel from His Book. This was when they had made a golden calf as an idol. God was very angry with the people to the point that Moses interceded for them.

Exodus records the following conversation:

> Now it came to pass on the next day that Moses said to the people, "You have committed a great sin. So now I will go up to the LORD; perhaps I can make atonement for your sin." Then Moses returned to the LORD and said, "Oh, these people have committed a great sin, and have made for themselves a god of gold! Yet, now, if you will forgive their sin—but if not, I pray, blot me out of Your book which You have written." And the LORD said to Moses, "Whoever has sinned against Me, I will blot him out of My book" (Exodus 32:30-33).

Of course we have all sinned and deserve to have our names blotted out of God's heavenly register. This is why we need the righteousness of Jesus. But this Scripture, as well as others, and history and experience, clearly teach us that not everyone who claims to be a believer has a personal relationship with God. This was certainly the situation at Sardis. Most of the people had their names on the "church rolls" but were not true believers. God's promise was not to them but to the overcoming remnant.

In the Book of Psalms, the writer urges God to blot out the names of the wicked from His book. Psalm 69:28 reads, *"Let them be blotted out of the book of the living, and not be written with the righteous."*

In Daniel, we learn that the persecution against the Jews during the tribulation period will be so severe that Michael, the guardian angel of Israel, will have to fight on their behalf. Yet God will deliver everyone whose name is written in the book. (See Daniel 12:1-3.)

The *pseudepigrapha* Book of First Enoch written between the Testaments in the Apocrypha mentions the same understanding and says that *"the names of* [the sinners] *shall be blotted out from the Book of Life"* (1 Enoch 108:3).

Since the New Testament is a Jewish book written by Jews, we should expect to find similar statements. Luke tells us that Jesus gave His disciples spiritual authority over demons. When the disciples rejoiced over their new power, Jesus rebuked them and reminded them of what was really important. He said, *"Nevertheless do not rejoice in this, that the spirits are subject to you, but rather rejoice because your names are written in heaven"* (Luke 10:20).

Paul wrote to the believers at Philippi:

> And I urge you also, true companion, help these women who labored with me in the gospel, with Clement also, and the rest of my fellow workers, whose names are written in the Book of Life (Philippians 4:3).

The writer of Hebrews encourages the believers with these words:

> But you have come to Mount Zion and the city of the living God, the heavenly Jerusalem, to an innumerable company of angels, to the general assembly and church [congregation] of the firstborn who are registered in heaven, to God the judge of all, to the spirits of just men made perfect (Hebrews 12:22-23).

In Revelation we learn that those who worship the Beast do not have their names written in God's heavenly register: *"All who dwell on the earth will worship him, whose names have not been written in the Book of Life of the Lamb slain from the foundation of the world"* (Rev. 13:8).

As it was at Sardis, there are millions of people today who profess Christianity but who do not have a personal relationship with the Lord. Their names are on the church roll but are not written in the Book of Life. The good news is that God knows the difference between those who profess Him and those who possess Him. God knows those who are His.

The prophet Nahum writes, *"The LORD is good, a stronghold in the day of trouble; and He knows those who trust in Him"* (Nah. 1:7).

The Apostle Paul quotes Nahum and writes to Timothy:

> *Nevertheless the solid foundation of God stands, having this seal: "The Lord knows those who are His," and, "Let everyone who names the name of Christ [Messiah] depart from iniquity"* (2 Timothy 2:19).

The third promise the Lord made to the faithful at Sardis is that He will acknowledge them before His Father and His angels. The small remnant of true believers were probably doing all they could to bring renewal to the congregation. But like in many of our modern traditional Christian denominations and local assemblies, their efforts were often not recognized nor appreciated. In spite of their best efforts, the entrenched leadership did not embrace their pleas for spiritual renewal.

The Son of Man gives His Word to the overcomers that He will acknowledge them. The Lord's promise is a combination of His statements recorded in Matthew and Luke. In the Matthew statement, Jesus says He will acknowledge His disciples before His Father in Heaven (see Matt. 10:32); while in the Luke passage He says He will acknowledge them before the angels of God (see Luke 12:8).

This is certainly an encouraging word to all of God's people who feel they are a struggling spiritual minority in their denomination or local congregation. The Lord Himself will acknowledge you as His own. What greater blessing and reward could we ever possibly desire than this?

Finally, as with all the other prophetic messages, Jesus says that we have a responsibility to listen to God's voice through the Holy Spirit. The fact that the Lord tells us to listen to hear His words means that He is still speaking to us today and that we can hear and understand His words.

The Lord speaks to each one of us personally based on our individual lives, much like parents would speak differently to their children based on their needs. As we obey what the Holy Spirit tells us, we overcome that need in our life and receive the promise God makes to us. Thus, the way we live now determines the glory that God has for us in the hereafter.

If the Lord's message to Sardis applies to your organization, your ministry, or your life, let us repent and do what He says so we can be overcomers. Let us heed the words of our Lord while we still have a little life: *"Blessed are those who hunger and thirst after righteousness, for they shall be filled"* (Matt. 5:6).

He who has an ear, let him hear.

REVIEW QUESTIONS

1. Write a summary of what you have learned in this lesson. Write the summary in clear concise words as if you are going to present it to another person.

2. Write an explanation of how you can apply what you have learned in this lesson to your life.

3. Share what you have learned with your family, friends, and members of your study group.

Chapter 11

The Letter to Philadelphia

REVELATION REVIEW

IF there was ever a congregation that needed a spiritual revival, it was the one at Sardis. While they must have had an exciting beginning, Jesus told them they were spiritually dead. This is why He greeted them as the One who has the seven Spirits of God, that is, the Holy Spirit.

God's life is in His Spirit. We must have an ongoing, fresh experience with the Holy Spirit in order to stay spiritually alive and vibrant. Jesus said that His followers would have rivers of living water flowing in them (see John 7:37-39). Can we honestly say that this describes our spiritual condition?

When Jesus spoke of living waters flowing in the believer's heart, He surely was referring to Jeremiah's words, *"They have forsaken Me, the fountain of living waters, and have hewn themselves cisterns—broken cisterns that can hold no water"* (Jer. 2:13; see also Jer. 17:13).

What is God talking about here? He is contrasting spiritual life that comes from a relationship with Him to dead religion. There is an infinite difference between having religion and having a relationship with

God. It is possible to have a religion about God without having a personal relationship with God.

In the Jeremiah verse, God mentions broken cisterns that do not hold water. God does not pour His life into a religion; He pours it into people. Religions are man's attempts to understand and explain God to people. But if the people who are in the religious organizations are not filled with God's Spirit, the organization becomes a broken cistern. It is also true of our individual lives. This is what God is meaning for us to understand through the words of the prophet.

When Jesus told the believers at Sardis that He knew their works, He was not giving them a compliment. He was giving them a warning. They had better wake up spiritually, or the little life they have left will be gone. The Lord does acknowledge a remnant in the congregation who still have some life. As with the other congregations, Jesus promises blessings to the overcomers, but has harsh words for those who fail to repent.

If there were such a thing as time travel, I would love to go back to the times in history when God caused great awakenings among His people. What an exciting privilege to witness and participate in the mighty moves of God that changed the world, such as when Luther realized that salvation was a free gift from God and not something we can earn. Or when God used John and Charles Wesley to preach their message of sanctification and holiness. Or to be at Azusa Street in 1906 when God poured out His Spirit in fresh manifestations of His power.

These mighty moves of God were birthed by men and women who were filled with God's Spirit to overflowing. The river of God's life poured out of them with such a force that God used them to change the world. God worked through them to create a movement of people responding to the outpouring of God's Spirit. These movements evolved into denominations that sought to carry on the vision of the spiritual pioneers they followed. Over time, these denominations evolved into religious organizations. Unfortunately, today, many of them are spiritually dead. This same process can happen in the life of local congregations as well as in our own lives. Let us accept Paul's admonition to *"be filled with the Spirit"* (Eph. 5:18).

My heart rejoices to share the Lord's letter to the believers at Philadelphia. The reason is because the Lord only had praise for them—no rebuke. Before reading His letter, let's learn about the history, geography, and archaeology of this ancient city.

BACKGROUND

On his next-to-last stop, the courier with the prophetic messages from God traveled about 28 miles southeast of Sardis to Philadelphia (not the one in Pennsylvania, USA). Philadelphia was located on the main Roman postal road at an important east-west and north-south junction. Situated on a high plateau, the city was about 100 miles inland from Smyrna, making it a gateway city to the east. Other than its important location at the junction, Philadelphia was not a large, influential town like the others where the Lord sent His letters.

It is interesting how Philadelphia got its name. Historians believe this came about at the time the city was founded. Eumenes was the king of Pergamos from 197-159 B.C. His brother who succeeded him was Attalus (159-138 B.C.), who was mentioned in a previous chapter. The Romans tried to cause a rivalry between the two brothers, but Attalus remained loyal to Eumenes. As a result, Eumenes started referring to his brother by the name *Philadelphus,* which in Greek means "brotherly love." When Eumenes and Attalus built the city, they named it as a witness to their relationship. As noted in Chapter 8, when Attalus died he did not have a successor, so he bequeathed his territory to the Romans in 133 B.C.

Philadelphia changed names several times. When Tiberius helped the city recover from an earthquake, the city elders renamed the town in honor of the emperor and called it *Neocaesarea.* Later, when the

Emperor Vespasian aided the city, they renamed it after him and called it *Flavia*.

Over the next centuries, Philadelphia embraced so many Greek gods and goddess it was known as "Little Athens." This is clear evidence that Byzantine Christianity was not able to convert the city from its paganisms. This must have been a real heartache for the believers. In view of these frequent changes, names were important to the small struggling community of believers at Philadelphia.

The ancient city is now called Alasehir, and has a population of about 40,000. About the only archaeological remains are those of a Byzantine Basilica.

The most important fact we need to know about the history of Philadelphia is that it was situated in an area where there were frequent and violent earthquakes. Philadelphia was destroyed in the A.D. 17 earthquake that destroyed Sardis, Laodicea, and other cities in the area. These and other cities in the area were destroyed by another earthquake in A.D. 60. Since the pagan temples were the only structures built to withstand earthquakes, the temples would be the most secure structure in the city. In a really severe earthquake, the pillars of the temples would be about the only thing left standing.

People who have lived through an earthquake tell us that the fear of anticipation of aftershocks is as unsettling to their souls as the aftershocks are to the land. The people in Philadelphia lived constantly with this fear.

After the earthquakes, the citizens of Philadelphia would leave the rubble of the city and go out into the nearby fields and live in tents. Then, when the tremors stopped and they rebuilt their homes, they would return to the city. So the people were always going in and coming out. We have witnessed this in our own times in places where there have been earthquakes and other natural disasters.

Volcanic soil is great for growing grapes. As a result, vineyards and winemaking was the main source of income for the city. In the chapter about Pergamos, I mentioned that Dionysus was considered the god of wine. He would have been the principal "god" at Philadelphia. Festivals and drunken revelry would have been held in his honor.

Now enough of the background. Let's see what the Son of Man had to say to the believers at Philadelphia and how He connected His words to their situation as citizens of this earthquake-prone city.

TO THE CONGREGATION AT PHILADELPHIA
(REVELATION 3:7-13)

The Greeting (verse 7)

As just mentioned, *Philadelphia* in Greek means "brotherly love." The word is found six additional times in the New Testament. (See Romans 12:10; First Thessalonians 4:9; Hebrews 13:1; First Peter 1:22; Second Peter 1:7.) How did the Lord greet His people who were living in the city of "brotherly love"? He makes two statements about Himself. First, He encourages them by reminding them that He is the One who is holy and true.

Unlike the many Greek gods and goddesses and Roman emperors, the God of Abraham, Isaac, and Jacob is holy and true. This means that He is altogether different from His creation and is the ultimate reality. And He is the only one who is perfect in these attributes. The Greek gods and goddesses all had human traits.

Later in the Book of Revelation, the overcomers in Heaven sang the song of Moses and the song of the Lamb. Here are the words to the song:

> *Great and marvelous are Your works, Lord God Almighty!*
> *Just and true are Your ways, O King of the saints! Who*

shall not fear You, O Lord, and glorify Your name? For You alone are holy. For all nations shall come and worship before You, for Your judgments have been manifested (Revelation 15:3-4).

As the divine Son of God, Jesus has the same attributes of His Father in Heaven. At His first coming, the angel Gabriel said to Mary:

The Holy Spirit will come upon you, and the power of the Highest will overshadow you; therefore, also, that Holy One who is to be born will be called the Son of God (Luke 1:35).

Then, at His second coming, John had a spiritual vision of the Lord and wrote:

Now I saw heaven opened, and behold, a white horse. And He who sat on him was called Faithful and True, and in righteousness He judges and makes war (Revelation 19:11).

Yes, Jesus is the perfect, holy, faithful, and true One. He has put His Spirit in His followers to empower us to so that we too can live a holy life that is faithful and true to Him. As Peter writes, "*...but as He who called you is holy, you also be holy in all your conduct, because it is written, 'Be holy, for I am holy' *" (1 Pet. 1:15-16).

In his second letter, Peter reminds us that the world as we know it is going to be purged with fire. Therefore, we should live holy and blameless lives as we draw near to His appearing. He writes:

But the day of the Lord will come as a thief in the night, in which the heavens will pass away with a great noise, and the elements will melt with fervent heat; both the earth and the works that are in it will be burned up.

Therefore, since all these things will be dissolved, what manner of person ought you to be in holy conduct and godliness, looking for and hastening the coming of the day of God, because of which the heavens will be dissolved, being on fire, and the elements will melt with fervent heat?

Nevertheless we, according to His promise, look for new heavens and a new earth in which righteousness dwells. Therefore, beloved, looking forward to these things, be diligent to be found by Him in peace, without spot and blameless (2 Peter 3:10-14).

Jesus also identifies Himself as the One who has the key of David, with which He can open and no person can shut, and He can shut and no person can open (see Rev. 3:7). What did He mean by this statement? Jesus was referencing an incident recorded by Isaiah in regard to the most trusted official to King Hezekiah. Here is what happened.

Shebna was the chief of staff for King Hezekiah. In this responsibility, he had the keys to the king's palace. No one could see the king without Shebna's approval. He was the one who opened and closed the doors to the king. Shebna had great authority, but it was a delegated authority and not his own. Yet he was filled with pride, and made a burial vault for himself in the fashion that was reserved for kings. The Lord was not pleased and judged Shebna because of his pride.

Isaiah explains:

Thus says the Lord GOD of hosts: "Go, proceed to this steward, to Shebna, who is over the house, and say: 'What have you here; and whom have you here, that you have hewn a sepulcher here, as he who hews himself a sepulcher on high, who carves a tomb for himself in a rock? Indeed, the LORD will throw you away violently, O mighty man, and will surely seize you. He will surely turn violently and toss you like a ball into a large country; there you shall die, and there your glorious chariots shall be the shame of your master's house. So I will drive you out of your office, and from your position he will pull you down'" (Isaiah 22:15-19).

The Lord then replaced Shebna with one more worthy. Eliakim took Shebna's place as Hezekiah's chief of Sstaff. He was given much glory and honor throughout the kingdom. Eliakim now had the keys to the kingdom of the House of David. He could open any door he wanted and lock any door he chose. He was the chief executive and administrator of the king's affairs.

As Isaiah explains:

Then it shall be in that day, that I will call My servant Eliakim the son of Hilkiah; I will clothe him with your robe and strengthen him with your belt; I will commit your responsibility into his hand. He shall be a father to the inhabitants of Jerusalem and to the house of Judah. The key of the house of David I will lay on his shoulder; so he shall open, and no one shall shut; and he shall shut, and no one shall open. I will fasten him as a peg in a secure place, and he will become a glorious throne to his father's house (Isaiah 22:20-23).

The Lord says that the key to the house or kingdom of David will lay on his shoulders. This is an interesting statement. To take in the full meaning of the phrase, we must understand the word picture and symbolism of keys.

In Bible times, keys were not small like they are in western culture. They were very large, made of wood, and worked with wooden pegs to fit corresponding holes in the lock which kept the door fastened. Because a key was large, it was difficult to carry in one's hand. Instead, it was carried on the shoulder and was the sign of official authority. Using Bible language, the person who had the keys of the kingdom on his shoulder was said to have the government on his shoulder.

Jesus uses this imagery to say that He is the One Isaiah spoke about in another passage:

> *For unto us a Child is born, unto us a Son is given; and the government will be upon His shoulder. And His name will be called Wonderful, Counselor, Mighty God, Everlasting Father, Prince of Peace. Of the increase of His government and peace there will be no end, upon the throne of David and over His kingdom, to order it and establish it with judgment and justice from that time forward, even forever. The zeal of the Lord of hosts will perform this* (Isaiah 9:6-7).

The Commendation (verse 8)

Like the persecuted believers at Smyrna, the Lord only has good things to say to the congregation at Philadelphia. He gives them no rebuke. While the doors of professional advancement and social acceptance may have been closed to them, the Lord promises to open the door of His Kingdom to them. And no local authority can close it. The clear implication is that entrance into the Kingdom of God is much more to be desired than entrance or acceptance into the pagan community at Philadelphia.

This Word is certainly relevant for us today. The time is coming, and is even now, when godly Bible believers will find the doors of professional advancement and social acceptance closed. We will be shut out by those in power who hate our holy lives, our faithfulness to God's Word, and our need to speak the truth in love. Yet, the Lord promises that if we seek first His Kingdom and His righteousness, He will open

His Kingdom doors to us and give us all that we need to fulfill our destiny (see Matt. 6:33).

The words of the psalmist are so appropriate to our times. He said, *"I would rather be a doorkeeper in the house of my God than dwell in the tents of wickedness...No good thing will He withhold from those who walk uprightly"* (Ps. 84:10-11).

Because they have not had much influence on the community, the congregation at Philadelphia apparently felt like a failure. But the Son of Man tells them that He knows their works and He commends them for three things. First, He encourages them by recognizing that they have a little strength. While this may not sound like a "glowing report," the Lord is acknowledging that they do have a measure of spiritual anointing, authority, and power. That is a good thing.

Like the believers at Philadelphia, we may sometimes feel as if we don't have much left in our spiritual gas tank. But the Lord is gracious and is always looking for something good in us that He can praise. Paul said it this way to the believers at Philippi: *"being confident of this very thing, that He who has begun a good work in you will complete it until the day of Jesus Christ* [Yeshua the Messiah]" (Phil. 1:6).

If you are feeling like you only have a little spiritual strength, don't be discouraged. We don't live by our feelings but by faith in God's faithfulness to finish the work He has started in us. If you are facing difficult challenges in your life and feel like you are not very spiritual, God will help you and give you the strength you need. As Paul said to the same believers at Philippi: *"for it is God who works in you both to will and to do for His good pleasure"* (Phil. 2:13).

Second, the Lord commends them because they have kept or obeyed His Word. God's Word is not just to be learned for the sake of getting information; it is to be obeyed. Many say that they love the Lord, but they don't do what He says. They are deceived and blind to their true spiritual condition. Jesus coupled loving Him with obeying Him. He told His disciples, *"If you love Me, keep My commandments....He who has My commandments and keeps them, it is he who loves Me..."* (John 14:15,21).

The believers at Philadelphia were not only learning God's Word, they were keeping God's Word. Sometimes believers today confuse knowing God's Word with keeping or obeying God's Word. Just because we know something doesn't mean we are doing it. We must get past the Western idea of learning for the sake of knowledge and learn for the sake of reverencing God and doing His Word.

In times when we may be persecuted for confessing our faith, knowledge without obedience may cause us more harm than good. In hard times we will be challenged to "practice what we preach." Christianity is much more than a doctrine. It is a way of life. We must have the spiritual resolve to "live the Word" and not just confess the Word. As James said, *"But be doers of the word, and not hearers only, deceiving yourselves"* (James 1:22).

Next, the Lord commends the believers at Philadelphia because they have not denied His name. After Jesus was resurrected and sent the Holy Spirit, His disciples did many miracles in and around Jerusalem. Because of this, thousands who witnessed the miracles and heard the name of Jesus proclaimed became His followers. This included a lame man Peter healed at the gate of the Temple. The high priest was infuriated. He had Peter and John brought before him so he could interrogate and intimidate them.

He ordered them not to preach, teach, or heal in the name of Jesus. Acts reads: *"So they called them and commanded them not to speak at all nor teach in the name of Jesus"* (Acts 4:18). Peter and John responded, *"Whether it is right in the sight of God to listen to you more than to God, you judge. For we cannot but speak the things which we have seen and heard"* (Acts 4:19-20).

When the high priest let Peter and John go, they continued their ministry in the name of Jesus. The Lord honored the preaching of His name and His Word and healed many people. Once again, the high priest arrested the disciples and interrogated them. Acts explains:

> And when they had brought them, they set them before the council. And the high priest asked them, saying, "Did we not strictly command you not to teach in this name? And look, you have filled Jerusalem with your doctrine, and intend to bring this Man's blood on us!" But Peter and the other apostles answered and said: "We ought to obey God rather than men" (Acts 5:27-29).

Before letting them go, the high priest beat the disciples and again commanded them not to speak in the name of Jesus. This did not deter the disciples, but made them even more determined, as we read:

> So they departed from the presence of the council, rejoicing that they were counted worthy to suffer shame for His name. And daily in the temple, and in every house, they did not cease teaching and preaching Jesus as the Christ [Messiah] (Acts 5:41-42).

As the governments of the world, including America, become more godless, the clash between light and darkness, good and evil, Judeo-Christianity and the New World Order will become more evident. There will be a repeat of the conflict we read about in the Book of Acts between the establishment and the people of God. We modern believers must be like the early disciples, the believers at Philadelphia, and God's holy remnant who have been persecuted throughout the ages. In the face of interrogation and intimidation, we must not deny our Lord. We must resolve now that when faced with the choice, we will obey God rather than man.

Jesus said:

Therefore whoever confesses Me before men, him I will also confess before My Father who is in heaven. But whoever denies Me before men, him I will also deny before My Father who is in heaven (Matthew 10:32-33).

We are blessed if the Lord counts us worthy to suffer for His name. God will give us the conviction, courage and strength to speak boldly of His name. As Peter wrote:

But even if you should suffer for righteousness sake, you are blessed. "And do not be afraid of their threats, nor be troubled." But sanctify the Lord God in your hearts, and always be ready to give a defense to everyone who asks you a reason for the hope that is in you, with meekness and fear (1 Peter 3:14-15).

The Promise (verses 9-13)

The Lord gives these faithful, struggling believers four incredible promises. First, He says that those who have opposed them will ultimately acknowledge that they are the true children of God. The Lord will vindicate them by confessing them before His Father in Heaven. Their tormentors will also make this confession. If people have spoken evil of you because of your life as a believer, the Lord will "get even for you." It will certainly be a sweet time of acknowledgment, recognition, and vindication for your faithfulness.

Jesus identifies the group that was persecuting the believers as belonging to the same group in Smyrna. They were both called the *"synagogue of satan"* (Rev. 2:9; 3:9), and they both claimed to be Jews but were not. I pointed out in the earlier discussion in Chapter 7 that there were then, as there are now, groups who claim to be Jews but are not Jews.

While it may be true that these are Jews, we really don't know who Jesus is talking about and cannot assume they are Jews. Whoever they were, they were claiming to be the chosen ones of God and were persecuting the followers of Jesus. It is interesting that archaeologists have never found any evidence of a synagogue in Philadelphia. However, there is an inscription from the third century that was found 10 miles east of the city referencing a "synagogue of the Hebrews."

Second, the Lord promises to keep them from the hour of trial which will come upon the whole earth to test those who dwell on the earth. This statement certainly seems to refer to the period of tribulation at the end of the age before the coming of Messiah. Those who teach a pre-tribulation rapture of believers use this verse to support their view. That would be nice, but after considering all the Scriptures plus the whole history of God's people, it is just wishful, Western thinking.

This is not merely my opinion. Jesus Himself used the same terminology and prayed to the Father, *"I do not pray that You should take them out of the world, but that you should keep them from the evil one"* (John 17:15). The Lord's words should be very clear to any of us who want to know truth rather than the religious teachings of men. He does not pray that believers be removed from the earth but that we are able to overcome the evil one. He is praying and then promises to protect His own from the wrath of God, which He will pour out on the earth.

Jesus used a similar phrase again when He taught His disciples how to pray. He said we should pray, *"And do not lead us into temptation, but deliver us from the evil one"* (Matt. 6:13). Is there any believer who has not been tempted by the evil one? Of course not; we all have. Clearly, Jesus is not saying that we will not be tempted, but that we should pray for God to help us overcome [be delivered from] the evil one. The second part of His statement clarifies the first part. To be delivered from the evil one means to *overcome* the evil one.

The Lord's promise is not that believers will be removed from the earth, but that He will protect us from the wrath of God and help us overcome the evil one by the blood of the Lamb and the word of our testimony (see Rev. 12:11). The Lord then tells them that when He does come, it will be quick or sudden. Therefore, they should hold fast to the little strength they have so that no one will take their crown.

Let's not be naïve. We live in a post Judeo-Christian world. Jesus said, *"In the world you will have tribulation; but be of good cheer, I have overcome the world"* (John 16:33).

The third promise is that He will make them a pillar in the temple of God and that they shall go out no more. The Lord is referring to the situation at Philadelphia when the earthquakes destroyed the city and the people had to go out to the fields and live in tents. As I explained earlier in this chapter, the only structures built to withstand the earthquakes were the pagan temples. And sometimes the pillars of the temples were the only structures to survive. There are many pillars of ancient structures still standing today. Also, the tents were only a temporary dwelling.

What the Lord wants them to know is that unlike the physical pillars in pagan temples, the people themselves will be the pillars in God's temple in His New Jerusalem. Of course, the Lord is using a figure of speech to help them understand His point. The people will not be literal pillars. Since God Himself will be with them, there will be no need for a physical temple in the New Jerusalem (see Rev. 21:22).

By relating to the physical situation of the city, Jesus used terminology that spoke of a sure foundation of permanence. There will be no earthquakes in the city of God. The people won't have to constantly come in and go out of God's city and live in temporary shelters. They will be safe and secure forever in God's presence in His eternal city.

The fourth promise is a threefold assurance that the Lord will place God's name on them, the name of His city on them, and His own new name on them. This is the Lord's way of saying in terms they would understand that the One True God is their God, and that they are His people forever. They belong to Him, are citizens of God's eternal city, the New Jerusalem, and the Lord will give them a new name that reflects their relationship with Him. This is an ancient way of communicating going all the way back to the Book of Numbers when God said He would put His name on the children of Israel and bless them. (See Numbers 6:22-27.)

It was the custom to write people's names on the pillars of public buildings and temples. For example, when Solomon built the temple in Jerusalem, he called two of the pillars after people's names. (See First Kings 7:21.)

Archaeologists have discovered many pillars bearing people's names, including pillars of temples. Jesus is encouraging the believers in Philadelphia. Because of their faithfulness, they will forever be God's people, living in His presence in His city that will never change names or be destroyed, and they will bear the likeness of the glorified Son of Man forever. Hallelujah!

If the Lord's message to Philadelphia applies to your organization, your ministry, or your life, find comfort in these words from Peter:

> *Blessed be the God and Father of our Lord Jesus Christ* [Yeshua the Messiah], *who according to His abundant mercy has begotten us again to a living hope through the resurrection of Jesus Christ* [Yeshua the Messiah] *from the dead, to an inheritance incorruptible and undefiled and that does not fade away, reserved in heaven for you, who are kept by the power of God through faith for salvation ready to be revealed in the last time* (1 Peter 1:3-5).

He who has an ear, let him hear.

REVIEW QUESTIONS

1. Write a summary of what you have learned in this lesson. Write the summary in clear concise words as if you are going to present it to another person.

2. Write an explanation of how you can apply what you have learned in this lesson to your life.

3. Share what you have learned with your family, friends, and members of your study group.

Chapter 12

The Letter to Laodicea

REVELATION REVIEW

THANK God for the believers at Philadelphia. They had some spiritual strength, they had kept God's Word, and they had not denied His name. No wonder the Lord made such incredible promises to them. Oh, that He would say that about us today.

The faithfulness of this little company of believers should be an example for us to imitate. Just think about their situation. They are living in a city that has so many Greek gods and goddesses it is called "Little Athens." Dionysus, the god of wine, is the chief deity at Philadelphia. Festivals to Dionysus were drunken orgies filled with every kind of debauchery imaginable. If they wanted, the city leaders could have Mardi Gras every day.

Furthermore, the citizens of Philadelphia lived in constant fear of an earthquake. They never knew when the next "big one" would hit. They had to have their camping gear handy just in case. They were always going in and out. Nothing was permanent. The believers at Philadelphia were truly living on shaky ground.

In spite of their many obstacles and challenges, the believers were faithful. This is the message for us today—faithfulness. Western Christians think of salvation by grace through faith. To our modern minds, faith is a noun, that is, it is a state of believing. It is passive, based on a mental agreement with certain religious teachings. In fact, the dictionary defines faith as "belief in God" or "a system of religious beliefs."

While this is how we normally think about the word *faith,* the Bible has a fuller meaning of the word. In the Bible, faith is not just a mental agreement or acceptance of certain religious teaching. It is not a passive word; it is an active word. It carries the meaning of steadfastness. The dictionary does include this larger understanding of the word *faith,* but it is not how we use the word in our everyday thinking and conversation.

In defining the meaning of faith, the dictionary also says that faith is fidelity to one's promises. In other words, faith is an active word that is a way of life. Faith is not just a state of believing with our minds; it is the steadfast allegiance, loyalty, and unwavering commitment to live our lives in accordance to what we believe. A person who is faithful is a person who is full of faith. They are "faith full."

We know this is how the Lord is using the word *faith* because He commends the congregation at Philadelphia for keeping His command to persevere (see Rev. 3:10). Because the believers at Philadelphia were faithful, the Lord promised to open the doors of His Kingdom to them, to preserve them in the great time of testing and tribulation, to avenge them against their enemies, and to give them permanence in His presence and in His holy city forever. May we live our lives in such a way that the Lord could make this promise to us. Amen!

What was happening in the city of Philadelphia that caused the Lord to say the things He said to these believers? The only way we can fully understand His letter is to learn about the history, geography and archaeology of this ancient city.

Background

I wonder what was going through his mind when God's special mailman set out from Philadelphia to Laodicea. He had heard John's letters read to each of the congregations. After delivering the Lord's prophetic messages to the first six congregations, he is now on his way to the last of the seven communities of believers.

Laodicea was about 130 miles inland and about 40 miles southeast of Philadelphia. It was located at a major east-west junction connecting the sea to the west to inland cities to the east. This strategic location helped make Laodicea a very prosperous city.

Laodicea was founded by Antiochus II around 260 B.C. He must have been a wise husband, since he named the city after his wife, Laodicea. The city had six unique characteristics that the Lord used to relate to the spiritual condition of the congregation.

First, Laodicea was a very wealthy city and the hub of banking and commerce in the region. We might think of it as the Wall Street of its geographic area. When Laodicea and the surrounding cities were destroyed in the earthquake of A.D. 60, Rome offered and gave financial assistance to help the cities rebuild. Laodicea was the only city in the region that refused to accept the aid. They considered themselves to be financially self-sufficient and didn't need Roman assistance. They had plenty of money to rebuild, with ample left over to spend on discretionary purchases. The city embodied the concept of "conspicuous consumption."

Second, Laodicea was famous for raising a special breed of sheep that was found nowhere else in the region. The sheep produced soft, shiny, raven-black wool that was in great demand and sold for a premium price. The production and sale of this wool contributed greatly to the employment and prosperity of the city. People would come from all over the region to buy this beautiful product and spend their money with the local merchants.

Third, Laodicea had a drinking problem. I don't mean alcohol, but water. Hierapolis, only six miles north of Laodicea, was famous for its hot mineral waters. People from all over the region would flock to Hierapolis to take baths, as they believed the hot mineral waters had therapeutic value. Colosse was only eight miles south of Laodicea and was known for its pure cold water, which was great for drinking. The Romans built an aqueduct to bring water from nearby sources to Laodicea. But by the time the water reached Laodicea, it was lukewarm and had a high concentration of mineral content. So it was not great drinking water. Hot water was good for bathing, and cold water was good for drinking. But lukewarm water with a high mineral concentration was not much good for anything. If there was any town that needed bottled water, it was Laodicea.

Because Laodicea, Hierapolis, and Colosse were so close to each other, they were considered a tri-city area. They were connected economically, socially, and spiritually. When the apostle Paul wrote his letter to the believers at Colosse, he mentioned Laodicea five times and Hierapolis once. (See Colossians 2:1; 4:13-16.) In fact, Paul mentions that he had written a letter to the congregation at Laodicea (see Col. 4:16). Now, that would make a good novel or movie: *The Lost Letter of Laodicea.*

Paul also commends Epaphras, who had come to Rome seeking Paul's advice on problems threatening the congregation at Colosse. Epaphras was from Colosse and may have started the congregation that met in Philemon's house (see Philem. 1:1-2) as well as the congregation at Laodicea. He ministered to the believers at Laodicea and Hierapolis (see Col. 4:12-13). Paul even tells us the name of the person in whose house the Laodicean believers met. He sends greetings to the brethren in Laodicea, and to Nymphas (masculine)—which probably should read Nympha (feminine)—and the church meeting in his (or her) house (see Col. 4:15). This was a small group of believers.

Fourth, Laodicea was an important center for the treatment of eye diseases. There was a temple dedicated to Asklepios, and a medical school and clinic that was a leader in the study and treatment of the eyes. One of the graduates of the school was a man named Demosthenes Philalethes, who was the most renowned ophthalmologist of his time. The medical school had developed a salve and powder for treating eyes that was produced and sold throughout the region. As a result, Laodicea was the medical center of the area, which made the city even more prosperous.

Fifth, because of its wealth, local Roman officials often abused their power and its hospitality, and forced the locals to buy them extra provisions such as clothing, food, or guest accommodations, or pay bribes or excessive taxes. Instead of respecting the locals, Roman officials violated common rules of hospitality, such as announcing themselves and knocking before entering. If they needed to "borrow" someone's estate for the evening, they wouldn't bother to knock or identify themselves. They would just barge right in and announce they were taking over. They requisitioned housing and lodging at will and took what they wanted.

Sixth, Laodicea was called a "throne city." In 40 B.C., Laodicea was attacked in an effort to overthrow the Romans. One of its citizens, named Zeno, along with his son, Polemo, held back the attackers. The Romans rewarded this family by making them kings over the area. Zeno and his son shared the throne and ruled as co-regents. Their descendants continued to rule for several generations and were featured on coins in the city.

Records indicate there was a sizable Jewish community at Laodicea that was assimilated and enjoyed the wealth that went with being a Laodicean. There is no record at this time of a synagogue or tension with the Christians in the city.

Ancient Laodicea lies in ruins near the modern city of Denizli, which has a population of about 200,000. Let's now read what the Lord has to say to His people at Laodicea.

TO THE CONGREGATION AT LAODICEA
(REVELATION 3: 14-22)

The Greeting (verse 14)

The Lord greets the congregation at Laodicea with three statements. First He says that He is the "Amen." The word *amen* basically means truth or reality. The word *verily* has the same meaning. In the King James Version, when Jesus would say, *"Verily I say unto you,"* He was emphasizing the absolute truth of His statement.

God is the God of truth. He is the God of the amen. Before the people crossed into the land, Moses taught them a song, part of which says, *"He is the Rock, His work is perfect; for all His ways are justice, a God of truth and without injustice; righteous and upright is He"* (Deut. 32:4).

When King David called on God to deliver him from his enemies, he prayed, *"Into Your hand I commit my spirit; You have redeemed me, O LORD God of truth"* (Ps. 31:5). Bible students recognize that Jesus quoted from this Scripture as He was about to die (see Luke 23:46). The Lord was able to trust that His Father would not let His body see corruption, nor His soul stay in *Sheol,* because His Father had given Him His Word of truth (see Ps. 16:10).

Since God is truth, His Word is truth for always and for all times. Psalm 119:89 tells us, *"Forever, O LORD, Your word is settled in heaven."* As Isaiah said, *"The grass withers, the flower fades, but the word of our God stands forever"* (Isa. 40:8). Jesus said, *"Heaven and earth will pass away, but My words will by no means pass away"* (Matt. 24:35).

The Hebraic understanding of the word *amen* is even more power-ful. The word *amen* consists of the Hebrew letters the Aleph, the Mem, and the Nun. In Hebrew, it is pronounced as *El/Mellech/N'eman*, which means, "God the faithful King."

Unlike the congregation at Laodicea, God is a faithful, covenant-keeping God. We can trust His Word as truth and trust Him to keep His Word. He has fully revealed His Word in human form in the person of Jesus who is the glorified Son of Man we see in the Book of Revelation. This is why Paul writes, *"For all the promises of God in Him are Yes, and in Him Amen, to the glory of God through us"* (2 Cor. 1:20).

Second, because the Lord is the "Amen," He is also the Faithful and True witness. In Revelation 1:5, Jesus introduced Himself as the Faith-ful Witness. In Revelation 19:11, He is called Faithful and True. These statements connect to Deuteronomy 18:18 where God says He will raise up a prophet like Moses. Unfortunately, the Laodiceans were not being faithful and true.

As the Faithful and True witness, we can trust the teachings and words of Jesus as recorded in the Bible. As He Himself said:

> For I have not spoken on My own authority; but the Father who sent Me gave Me a command, what I should say and what I should speak. And I know that His com-mand is everlasting life. Therefore, whatever I speak, just as the Father has told Me, so I speak (John 12:49-50).

The writer of Hebrews says it this way:

> God, who at various times and in various ways spoke in time past to the fathers by the prophets, has in these last days spoken to us by His Son, whom He has appointed heir of all things, through whom also He made the worlds (Hebrews 1:1-2).

Plato said, "We must lay hold of the best of human opinion in order to sail over the dangerous sea of life; unless we can find a stronger boat or some sure Word of God which will more surely and safely carry us." We have found that sure Word of God in written and human form.

Third, the Lord says that He is *"the Beginning of the creation of God"* (Rev. 3:14). In this statement, Jesus does not mean that He was created. The phrase means that He is the heir of creation. Paul made the same statement in his letter to the believers at Colosse. He said of Jesus, *"He is the image of the invisible God, the firstborn over all creation"* (Col. 1:15).

We have already learned that Paul's letter to the Colossians was also read to the believers at Laodicea. They both would have understood Paul and Jesus to mean that Jesus is the firstborn or heir of creation.

The phrase refers to the custom in ancient times of the father of the family choosing one of his sons to be his heir. It was usually the oldest son, but not always. For example, Esau was born first, but his father Isaac did not choose him as the firstborn. Isaac chose Jacob to be the firstborn. The phrase "firstborn" is actually a title of the one who received the inheritance and priestly responsibilities of the family. The firstborn is given a double portion of the family resources and becomes the priest and spiritual head of the family.

God chose His son Jesus to be the firstborn or heir of creation. Psalm 2 says it this way:

> *I will declare the decree: the LORD has said to Me, "You are My Son, Today I have begotten You* [made You heir]. *Ask of Me, and I will give You the nations for Your inheritance, and the ends of the earth for Your possession"* (Psalm 2:7-8).

The Rebuke (verses 15-19)

Unfortunately, as with Sardis, the Lord did not have anything praiseworthy to say to the congregation at Laodicea. Instead of living as salt and light, the community of believers had assimilated into the lifestyle of the city.

Jesus relates their spiritual condition to the condition of the city. He rebukes them for being lukewarm in their faith and commitment. The hot mineral springs at Hierapolis were good for medicinal purposes. The cold water springs at Colosse were good for drinking purposes. But the lukewarm, mineral-laden water at Laodicea was nauseating. When you took a drink, you had to hold your nose because of the smell, and you almost regurgitated when you swallowed it. Yuk!

This rebuke of being lukewarm may not be what we might think. It is not that the believers weren't doing anything, but that the Lord did not approve of their efforts. They were lukewarm toward Him. They were relying on their own self-sufficiency rather than trusting God. Because they had money, they did not see a need to rely on God. They thought they were spiritual and were doing good works because they were using their money for "the work of the church" or for the "ministry." The Lord says their works are tasteless to Him and that He will spit them out of His mouth as the Laodiceans often did with their bad water.

The Lord says that, spiritually speaking they are wretched, miserable, poor, blind, and naked. WOW! These are words that describe a beggar. In their eyes, they were rich, but in God's eyes, they were spiritually poor.

The believers had prospered along with the city. Now, there is nothing wrong with God's people prospering. It is a good thing. The Bible is clear that God desires to bless His people with financial resources. Poverty is not a blessing from God. But at Laodicea, the people were trusting in their wealth rather than in God who is the giver of wealth.

The congregation had the same attitude of self-sufficiency demonstrated by the city. Because of its affluence, the city did not need help from Rome to rebuild after the earthquake of A.D. 60. Likewise, the congregation put their trust in their wealth. In their minds, they did not need the Lord to help them build their community. They had their money. While it is good that they were blessed financially, it was tragic that they did not see their need for spiritual blessings. They had not learned to trust God, because, in their minds, they didn't need to do so.

Sadly, there are many Laodicean congregations and believers today. Generally speaking, God has blessed American Christians with financial resources. Most have a job, a checking account, and some savings. They can pay their bills, take vacations, and eat at nice restaurants. This is good. Compared to most people in the world, American believers have plenty.

Many think they are spiritual because they give to the building program, the "work of the church," or to ministries, or help the poor. But they have never seen the need to trust and rely on God or truly operate in faith, because they have money in the bank. Just as it is easy to trust God for healing when we are not sick, it is easy to trust God for resources we already have. This does not take faith. And without faith it is impossible to please God (see Heb. 11:6).

The Lord counsels the congregation at Laodicea to do three things, and relates each to the situation in the city. First, in order to be truly rich, He counsels them to buy gold refined in the fire. Does He mean literal gold? Because of inflation and the depreciating value of the dollar, many financial advisers counsel people to buy gold. Is this what the Lord meant?

The gold the Lord wants them to buy is genuine faith in God that has been refined through the challenges of life. Jesus said it is His gold that we get from Him, not from the gold merchants. God's gold of faith comes from Him and is the true riches. Peter explains:

> *In this you greatly rejoice, though now for a little while, if need be, you have been grieved* [distressed] *by various trials, that the genuineness of your faith, being much more precious than gold that perishes, though it be tested by*

*fire, may be found to praise, honor, and glory at the rev-
elation of Jesus Christ* [Messiah] (1 Peter 1:6-7).

If the American economy continues to crumble, believers who have
put their trust in their finances rather than in the Lord will be devastated unless they learn to put their trust in God. Peter adds:

> ...*knowing that you were not redeemed with corrupt-
> ible things, like silver or gold, from your aimless conduct
> received by tradition from your fathers, but with the pre-
> cious blood of Christ* [Messiah], *as of a lamb without
> blemish and without spot. He indeed was foreordained
> before the foundations of the world, but was manifest in
> these last times for you who through Him believe in God,
> who raised Him from the dead and gave Him glory, so
> that your faith and hope are in God* (1 Peter 1:18-21).

The second counsel the Lord gives them is to buy white garments
from Him to cover their naked souls. Once again, the people were boast-
ing in their expensive designer garments made with the rich black wool.
Even though they wore pricey garments, the Lord warns them that they
are spiritually naked. The white garment symbolizes the garment of salvation and robe of righteousness that only the Lord can provide. He is
the designer and the only merchant of this heavenly garment.

The application for believers today should be obvious. With all of
our material prosperity, many denominations, local congregations, and
professing believers are spiritually naked. Their literal closets may be
full of nice clothes, but their spiritual closet is empty. They glory in their
financial independence, token religious activities, and spiritual talk, but
they are self-righteous and naked before God.

The third counsel the Lord gives is that they should anoint their
eyes with eye salve so they can see. As with His other statements, when
the people heard this warning, they knew exactly what the Lord meant.

While the Laodiceans had the leading medical center for healing of their eyes, they were spiritually blind. They could not see past the material world into the spiritual world. Their material prosperity and self-sufficiency clouded their spiritual vision.

Paul's prayer for the believers at Ephesus was that "the eyes of their understanding be enlightened" (see Eph. 1:18). This phrase expresses what Jesus meant for the Laodiceans. He wanted them to have "the eyes of faith" to see and understand spiritual riches, wisdom, and priorities.

The Laodiceans had what we might call "a religious spirit." They were religious, self-sufficient, and in need of nothing. They were blinded to their true spiritual state of being. Yet the Lord tells them that their spiritual condition is just the opposite of what they think of themselves. His final warning to them is tempered with the statement that He loves them (as family, with brotherly love) and because He loves them, He will rebuke (expose) and chasten (judge and discipline) those in the congregation that are truly His. If they are wise, they will eagerly receive His Words and repent.

God is a God of mercy who gives His people the opportunity to judge and correct themselves. Yet, if they fail to examine themselves and repent, God will judge them corporately and individually as is appropriate. This is because God loves us and wants us to be holy more than He wants us to be happy.

Paul explains this for us:

> For if we would judge ourselves, we would not be judged. But when we are judged, we are chastened by the Lord, that we may not be condemned with the world (1 Corinthians 11:31-32).

It is much easier and less painful to judge ourselves than for God to have to judge us. When we judge ourselves, our sins and the correction required is private between us and God. But when God judges us, He exposes our failings publicly. We already see this in the formal organized American Church, which has lost its way and is spiritually poor, blind, and naked.

The Promise (verses 20-22)

When Jesus was on the earth, He said, *"For where two or three are gathered together in My name, I am there in the midst of them"* (Matt. 18:20). The tragedy of the Laodicean congregation is that the Lord is not in their midst. They are "having church," but Jesus is not even there. The greater tragedy is that they don't even know He is not present with them. They are so self-sufficient, they can follow their programs and continue having services without the Lord.

Unlike the Roman officials who barged their way into homes, Jesus says that He is standing outside the door and knocking. This is the Lord's way of saying in words they could understand that He will not break down the door in a forced entry to the congregation or into our hearts. His love is extended to them, but they must recognize their need and invite His presence into their gatherings and into their lives.

Because of the hardness of their hearts, their self-sufficiency, and their complacency, not everyone will hear nor recognize the Lord's voice speaking to them. In John 10:27 Jesus said, *"My sheep hear My voice, and I know them, and they follow Me."*

We can hear and recognize the voice of the Lord speaking to us. In Bible times, when someone knocked at the door of your house and you asked who was there, they would not give their name. They would say, "It is I." You had to be able to recognize the person's voice or you would not open the door for them. This was the ancient "home alarm security system."

We have an example of this in the Book of Acts. Peter had been arrested and put in prison. But the Lord sent an earthquake and set him free. Peter went to the house where the disciples were praying, but found that the door was locked. He knocked on the door and waited for someone to open it and let him in.

Luke tells the story:

> *And as Peter knocked at the door of the gate, a girl named Rhoda came to answer. When she recognized Peter's voice, because of her gladness she did not open the gate, but ran in and announced that Peter stood before the gate. But they said to her, "You are beside yourself!" Yet she kept insisting that it was so. So they said, "It is his angel." Now Peter continued knocking; and when they opened the door and saw him, they were astonished* (Acts 12:13-16).

Rhoda recognized Peter's voice. He didn't say, "It is Peter." She knew his voice because she knew him. When Jesus stands outside the door knocking, He doesn't say, "It is Jesus." His people will recognize His voice and let Him into their lives. Those who don't know Him will not recognize His voice and will not let Him into their denominations, congregations, or personal lives.

To those who do know His voice and let Him into their lives, the Son of Man makes a wonderful promise. He says, *"I will come in to him and dine with him, and he with Me"* (Rev. 3:20). Now, this doesn't mean that the Lord will take you to your favorite restaurant. In Bible times, eating together was a sign of friendship and fellowship. To those in the Laodicean congregation who heard his voice, opened the door, and repented of their materialistic self-sufficiency, the Lord would commune with them. They would enjoy His presence, His power, and His provision.

Finally, to the overcomer, the Lord further promises that he will sit with Him on His throne, meaning that he will share in His rule over the nations. When the Lord returns, He will not only sit on the throne of His father David in Jerusalem as King of Israel. He will also sit on the throne of His heavenly Father as King of kings and Lord of lords. He will rule the nations as God's earthly representative. And His covenant people will rule with Him.

Jerusalem will be the ultimate "throne city" and the final home of God's people. Jeremiah tells us that Jerusalem will be called the throne of God (see Jer. 3:17). Daniel gives us the following prophetic words of hope when Messiah reigns on the earth:

> *I was watching in the night visions, and behold, One like the Son of Man, coming with the clouds of heaven! He came to the Ancient of Days, and they brought Him near before Him. Then to Him was given dominion and glory and a kingdom, that all peoples, nations, and languages should serve Him. His dominion is an everlasting dominion, which shall not pass away, and His kingdom the one which shall not be destroyed.*
>
> *...Then the kingdom and dominion, and the greatness of the kingdoms under the whole heaven, shall be given to the people, the saints of the Most High. His kingdom is an everlasting kingdom, and all dominions shall serve and obey Him* (Daniel 7:13-14,27).

If the Lord's message to Laodicea applies to your organization, your ministry, or your life, let us repent and do what He says so we can be overcomers. Let us heed the following words of Jesus:

> *Therefore do not worry, saying, "What shall we eat?" or "What shall we drink?" or "What shall we wear?" For after all these things the Gentiles seek. For our heavenly Father knows that you need all these things. But seek first the kingdom of God and His righteousness, and all these things shall be added to you* (Matthew 6:31-33).
>
> *He who has an ear, let him hear.*

Ancient Letters Still Speak Today

We began this book by noting that the Book of Revelation is about the glorious Son of Man who sits on His throne in Heaven at the right hand (place of honor) of His Father. Because of the suffering and tribulation faced by His people in the first century, Jesus sent a prophetic message to the seven congregations in Asia Minor. He chose to reveal His messages to John, who experienced an apocalyptic vision by which He received and recorded the words of the Lord.

In each message, Jesus reminded them that He knew of their works, praised them when He could, exhorted them and warned them of their failures, and promised incredible blessings to those who heard His Word, obeyed His Word and overcame.

While these messages were given to seven literal congregations of the first century, they are certainly relevant for God's people today. The world still rejects the rule of God, and human nature is the same. We still face the challenges of losing our first-love zeal for the Lord; overcoming fear in the midst of persecution; holding fast to true biblical faith and sound doctrine; and resisting moral compromise, spiritual deadness, worldliness, materialism, self-sufficiency, apathy, and blindness to our own spiritual need.

With the world becoming more and more anti-Judeo-Christian, our challenge is to hear what God is saying to His corporate community of believers and to our lives personally, and how to face an uncertain future with faith and confidence that God's Word is true. While God is already judging the nations and those who have fallen away from the faith, His promises are "Yes and Amen" to those who overcome.

As we face the future of living in an anti-God world, let us have the conviction and courage *not* to "fix our sandals" before the gods of government and the new world order. Let us not compromise for the sake of convenience and comfort and a false sense of security and materialism. But let us overcome by the blood of the Lamb and the word of our testimony. He that has an ear let him hear what the Spirit is saying to us today.

I hope you will continue in this study of the Book of Revelation by reading Volume Two in this series, which is entitled *The Lamb and the Seven-Sealed Scroll* and Volume Three entitled, *The Victorious Kingdom.*

May our glorious Lord help you be a faithful overcomer. May you live each day to the fullest with a joyous expectation of the good that He has promised. Until He comes, may our Father in Heaven grant you, according to the riches of His glory, to be strengthened with might through His Spirit in your inner man. May he constantly abide in your heart through faith. My you be so rooted and grounded in Him that you will comprehend and experience His infinite love for you. May you be filled with the fullness of God.

PROMISES TO THE OVERCOMERS

Meditate on these promises and let God's Spirit reveal to your spirit the glorious Son of Man. See what John saw and be blessed. The overcomers will…

- Eat of the tree of life.

- Not be hurt by the second death.

- Eat the hidden manna of the life of God.

- Receive a white stone of acceptance with a new name.

- Have power over the nations.

- Rule with the Lord with a rod of iron.

- Receive the Bright and Morning Star.

- Be clothed in white garments.

- Have their names written in the Book of Life.

- Hear the Lord confess their names as His own before His Father and the angels.

- Be a pillar in the Temple of God.

- Receive a new name to manifest the glory of God forever.

- Sit with Messiah on His throne.

REVIEW QUESTIONS

1. Write a summary of what you have learned in this lesson. Write the summary in clear concise words as if you are going to present it to another person.

2. Write an explanation of how you can apply what you have learned in this lesson to your life.

3. Share what you have learned with your family, friends, and members of your study group.

Bibliography

Booker, Richard. *The End of All Things is at Hand? Are You Ready?* Alachua, FL: Bridge-Logos, 2008.

Booker, Richard. *The Shofar: Ancient Sound of the Messiah.* Houston, TX: Sounds of the Trumpet, Inc., 1999.

Booker, Richard. *Here Comes the Bride: Ancient Jewish Wedding Customs and the Messiah.* Houston, TX: Sounds of the Trumpet Inc., 1995.

Booker, Richard. *Ancient Jewish Prayers and the Messiah.* Houston, TX: Sounds of the Trumpet Inc., 2003.

Charlesworth, James, editor. *The Old Testament Pseudepigrapha: Apocalyptic Literature & Testaments Volume 1.* New York: Doubleday, 1983.

DeMoss, Nancy Leigh, editor. *The Rebirth of America,* Philadelphia: Author S. DeMoss Foundation, 1986.

Fleming, Jim. *Understanding the Revelation.* Bellaire, TX: Biblical Resources, 1999.

Hemer, Colin J. *The Letters to the Seven Churches of Asia in their Local Setting.* Grand Rapids, MI: Eerdmans, 2001.

Ladd, George Eldon. *A Theology of the New Testament*. Grand Rapids, MI: Eerdmans, 1993.

Online Sources: Numerous well-researched articles on Greek mythology and the history, geography and archaeology of the seven cities in Asia Minor.

Osborne, Grant, general editor. *Life Application Bible Commentary: Revelation*. Carol Stream, IL: Tyndale House, 2000.

Wilson, Mark, Arnold, Clinton, editor. *Zondervan Illustrated Bible Backgrounds Commentary: Revelation*. Grand Rapids, MI: Zondervan, 2002.

Tenney, Merrill. *Interpreting Revelation*. Grand Rapids, MI: Eerdmans, 1970.

Stern, David H. *Jewish New Testament Commentary*. Clarksville, MD: Jewish New Testament Publications, 1992.

Varner, William. *Jacob's Dozen: A Prophetic Look at the Tribes of Israel*. Bellmawr, NJ: The Friends of Israel Gospel Ministry, 1987.

Walters, Brent. *Ante-Nicene Christianity: The First Three Centuries*. San Jose, CA: The Ante-Nicene Archive, 1993.

About Dr. Richard Booker

D R. Richard Booker, MBA, Ph.D., is an ordained Christian minister, President of Sounds of the Trumpet, Inc., and the Founder/Director of the Institute for Hebraic-Christian Studies. Prior to entering the ministry, he had a successful business career. He is the author of 35 books, numerous Bible courses, and study materials, which are used by churches and Bible schools around the world.

Dr. Booker has traveled extensively for over 30 years, teaching in churches and at conferences on various aspects of the Christian life as well as Bible prophecy, Israel, and the Hebraic roots of Christianity. He and his wife Peggy have led yearly tour groups to Israel for over 25 years. For 18 years, Dr. Booker was a speaker at the Christian celebration of the Feast of Tabernacles in Jerusalem. This gathering is attended by 5,000 Christians from 100 nations.

Dr. Booker and Peggy founded the Institute for Hebraic-Christian Studies (IHCS) in 1997 as a ministry to educate Christians in the Hebraic culture and background of the Bible, to build relationships between Christians and Jews, and to give comfort and support to the people of Israel. Their tireless work on behalf of Christians and Jews has been recognized around the world, as well as by the Knesset Christian Allies Caucus in Jerusalem.

Dr. Booker is considered a pioneer and spiritual father and prophetic voice in teaching on Bible prophecy, radical Islam, Israel, Jewish-Christian relations, and the biblical Hebraic roots of Christianity. He has made over 400 television programs, which can be seen worldwide on God's Learning Channel. To learn more about his ministry, see his Web site and online bookstore at www.rbooker.com. If you want to invite Dr. Booker to speak at your congregation or conference, you may contact him at shofarprb@aol.com.

IN THE RIGHT HANDS, THIS BOOK WILL CHANGE LIVES!

Most of the people who need this message will not be looking for this book. To change their lives, you need to put a copy of this book in their hands.

> *But others (seeds) fell into good ground, and brought forth fruit, some a hundred-fold, some sixty-fold, some thirty-fold* (Matthew 13:8).

Our ministry is constantly seeking methods to find the good ground, the people who need this anointed message to change their lives. Will you help us reach these people?

> *Remember this—a farmer who plants only a few seeds will get a small crop. But the one who plants generously will get a generous crop* (2 Corinthians 9:6).

EXTEND THIS MINISTRY BY SOWING
3 BOOKS, 5 BOOKS, 10 BOOKS, OR MORE TODAY,
AND BECOME A LIFE CHANGER!

Thank you,

Don Nori Sr., Founder
Destiny Image
Since 1982